1/03

ALSO BY DAVID ROBERTS

DAVID ROBERTS

SIMON & SCHUSTER

NEW YORK   LONDON   TORONTO   SYDNEY   SINGAPORE

ESCAPE FROM LUCANIA

AN EPIC STORY OF SURVIVAL

SIMON & SCHUSTER
Rockefeller Center
1230 Avenue of the Americas
New York, NY 10020

For information about special discounts for bulk purchases,
please contact Simon & Schuster Special Sales:
1-800-456-6798 or business@simonandschuster.com

Designed by Karolina Harris
Map copyright Jeff Ward

Manufactured in the United States of America

10 9 8 7 6 5 4 3 2 1

Library of Congress Cataloging-in-Publication Data

Roberts, David, 1943–
Escape from Lucania ; an epic story of survival / David Roberts.
p.   cm.
1. Mountaineering—Yukon Territory—Lucania, Mount—History. I. Title.
GV199.44.C22 Y848 2002
796.52'2'097191—dc21   2002073349

ISBN 0-7432-2432-9

Credits: All photos by Bradford Washburn except as noted.

To Bob and Brad—

Still fast and light in their nineties

CONTENTS

ESCAPE FROM LUCANIA

Route of Bates and Washburn,
June 18–July 19, 1937

July 12:
Cache destroyed by bears

WOLF CREEK
(STEELE) GLACIER

SAINT ELIAS RANGE

July 11:
Mount Steele

July 6:
Shangri-La

WALSH GLACIER

SPRING GLACIER

July 9:
Mount Lucania

June 18–22, 1937:
Base camp and stranded plane

DONJEK GLACIER

0 Miles   10

0 Kilometers   10

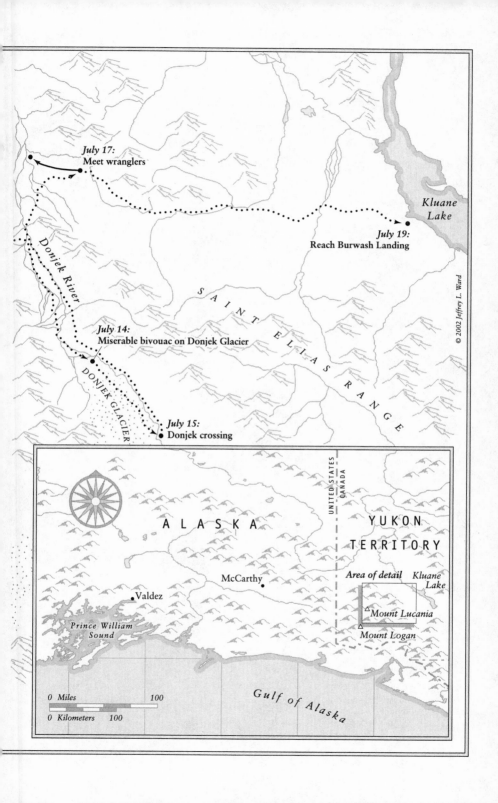

July 17:
Meet wranglers

Kluane Lake

July 19:
Reach Burwash Landing

© 2002 Jeffrey L. Ward

Donjek River

S A I N T E L I A S R A N G E

July 14:
Miserable bivouac on Donjek Glacier

DONJEK GLACIER

July 15:
Donjek crossing

UNITED STATES
CANADA

A L A S K A

Y U K O N

T E R R I T O R Y

McCarthy

Valdez

Area of detail *Kluane Lake*

Prince William Sound

△ *Mount Lucania*

△ *Mount Logan*

0 Miles   100
0 Kilometers   100

Gulf of Alaska

PROLOGUE

OPPOSITE me, upright in their adjoining armchairs, sat the two ninety-year-olds. Bald on top, with wisps of white hair crowning his ears, the aquiline nose and jutting chin proclaiming a lifetime of adamantine purpose, Henry Bradford Washburn, Jr., wore a brown dinner jacket over his red-plaid shirt, gray slacks, and canvas-and-rubber boots of the same make he had favored as a youth. His folded glasses were tucked into his shirt pocket. To Washburn's right, his hairline checked in mid-recession, black strands still mingled with gray, the creases around his eyes etched deep in his round face, Robert Hicks Bates wore a green-checked jacket, threadbare gray sweater, and gray slacks that might have come from the same surplus store as his friend's.

Both men looked frail, and both were a little hard of hearing. Approaching those armchairs, both men had walked with a slight stoop. Neither, I was sure, had gained a pound since his college days; perhaps they had each shrunk half an inch since their prime. The calm of a winter's afternoon reigned in the living room of Bates's second-floor apartment in this retirement community in Exeter, New Hampshire. A drab gray light flooded through south- and west-facing windows. Bob's wife of forty-seven years, Gail, served us tea and pound cake.

I watched the men talk as much as I listened to them. Brad's forehead wrinkled as he stabbed the air with his right index finger to emphasize a point. Bob sat with his hands clasped like a preacher, his eyes squinting almost shut as he grinned in memory. Brad's pronouncements came in cadenced, gravelly tones. Bob spoke in a soft, oddly high-pitched voice, delivering qualified comments on Brad's categorical judgments. Everything about the pair bespoke the comfort in each other's presence of two men who had been best friends for more than six decades.

As they chatted, I slipped into a reverie. Floating back sixty-four years in time, I saw Brad, at twenty-seven, lying head-to-toe with Bob, then twenty-six, as the pair shared a single sleeping bag in a wind-lashed tent at 14,000 feet in the heart of a glaciated wilderness in the Canadian Yukon. At that moment in 1937, there were no other human beings within eighty miles. A freak of nature had intersected with the men's intense ambition to land them here, on this high subarctic ridge where no one had ever been before, reduced to that cramped bivouac in a single bag. Most mountaineers, ensconced in such a predicament, would have dreaded the life-

and-death struggle that was about to ensue. But in my mind's eye, as they lay there cooking a dinner of Ovaltine, while the gale rattled the canvas that sheltered them from insupportable cold, both Brad and Bob had the blithe, insouciant look on their faces of pals sharing a fine adventure.

In that lonely camp, the men were five miles east of and 3,000 feet below the summit of Mount Lucania, one of the most remote peaks on the continent. In 1937, moreover, Lucania was the highest unclimbed mountain in North America. It had been attempted only once before, by a strong party in 1935 that, turning back from another summit ten miles away, had declared Lucania "impregnable." That gauntlet thrown before their feet was the challenge that had brought Brad and Bob to the Yukon. Neither man, however, could have foreseen the insidious handicap with which fate would shackle them before allowing them to clutch at their prize.

During the 105 years since a team led by an Italian nobleman, the Duke of the Abruzzi, made the daring first ascent of 18,008-foot Mount Saint Elias, the fourth-highest peak in North America, there have been scores of truly extraordinary climbs pulled off in the wilds of Alaska and the Yukon. Because of its peculiar circumstances, however, the 1937 Lucania expedition remains unique. As I sat in Bob Bates's living room, half-listening to the two old cronies reminisce, I mused that if I had to choose the single boldest deed in all that glorious history of northern ascent, I would vote for Bates and Washburn's assault on Mount Lucania.

I had first met Brad thirty-nine years before, Bob a year or two after that. Both men had gone to Harvard in 1929, where they had met at the beginning of their sophomore year. At nineteen, Brad had under his belt a remarkable record as a teenage climber in the Alps; with a famous French guide, he had made a major first ascent on the Aiguille Verte above Chamonix. Bob, on the other hand, had done little more than hike in New Hampshire's White Mountains before college.

At the time, the Harvard Mountaineering Club comprised the most ambitious collection of undergraduate mountaineers of any college or university in the country. Their specialty was remote, unclimbed peaks in Alaska and Canada. HMC climbers had done noteworthy things in the late 1920s, but it would be Bates and Washburn's generation—a small cadre of friends who pulled off first ascents in the great ranges all through the '30s and '40s and even into the '50s—that changed the face of American mountaineering.

When I went to Harvard myself in the fall of 1961, joining the HMC a few weeks after I arrived in Cambridge, the legacy of Bates and Washburn's crowd hung over the club. As ambitious in our own way as they had been in the 1930s, we too turned our sights toward unclimbed routes in Alaska and Canada. Nor was the presence of the earlier generation merely a matter of disembodied legends looking sternly down upon us from the hallowed rafters of their achievements. A number of the renowned oldsters attended our meetings and served on the HMC's Advisory Council. Henry Hall, who had founded the club in the basement of his family's Coolidge Hill house in 1924, and who the next year had participated in the epochal first ascent of Mount Logan in the Yukon (the second-highest peak in North America), was unfailingly present at every meeting, piping up in his Boston Brahmin tones during slide shows to correct an undergraduate's misidentification of some obscure peak in the Selkirk Range.

As the founding director of Boston's Museum of Science, however, Washburn was too busy to attend our meetings. Thus I did not meet him until halfway through my sophomore year. Seven of us HMCers had decided to climb Mount McKinley. At the age of nineteen, invited by a pair of seniors who were vastly more experienced than I, I felt overwhelmed but flattered by their vote of confidence. At the same time, the prospect of climbing North America's highest mountain scared the hell out of me.

Only one of our seven had been on an expeditionary mountain before. With ambitions tempered to match our experience, we pondered making the second ascent of McKinley's southeast spur.

Sometime during the winter, Washburn got wind of our plans and invited us over to his house on Sparks Street in Cambridge. By 1962, at the age of fifty-two, he had ceased to climb seriously, but during the previous three decades he had turned a hobby—making large-format black-and-white aerial photographs of Alaskan mountains—into an oeuvre so magisterial that he would come to be acclaimed, with the Italian Vittorio Sella, as one of the two greatest mountain photographers of all time.

Hardly bothering to introduce himself, Brad pulled us into his kitchen, where he slapped down photos of McKinley on the tabletop. Over the years he had made many flights around the mountain, which he had been the first man to climb three times. Brad waved off our notions of the southeast spur and insisted that we survey the north face, called the Wickersham

Wall after a Fairbanks judge who had attempted the mountain in 1903. The tallest precipice in North America—14,000 feet from the base to the north summit—the wall was still unclimbed. A team of Canadian veterans was planning a rather circuitous assault on the Wickersham, far out on its western edge, for the next summer; but Brad bade us look at a direct route up a shallow arête that split the huge face like a vector.

We peered at the photos, then, nervously, at each other. Washburn's ambitions for us seemed wildly grandiose: the route looked terrifying. Sensing our unease, he laid a pair of photos side by side, then unfolded a stereo viewer and plopped it down athwart the pictures. When we looked through the viewer, the mountain leapt out in three dimensions. "You get god-awful avalanches off the Wickersham," Brad said, "but that rib'll divide 'em right and left. I guarantee you it's a safe route. You better grab it before someone else does."

In thirty-five days, we hiked in to the mountain from the Denali Highway, climbed the Wickersham by its beautiful central arête, traversed over the north and south summits and down the West Buttress, circled back to base camp on the Peters Glacier, and hiked out. We had had a rollicking good time, and the route proved well within our abilities. The only close call came fording the flood-swollen McKinley River on the way out, only two hours before we reached the road.

During five days in July, however, as we holed up at 17,000 feet in a blizzard, our bush pilot became worried about us. He flew through the storm and then spotted our tracks thousands of feet below our camp, disappearing, he said, into avalanche debris. (The slides had struck long after we had passed that way, but our pilot had had no way of knowing that.) He put out a distress call. We made national headlines, and newscasters Huntley and Brinkley reported us missing and feared dead. In the midst of the furor, reporters interviewed Washburn. As confident as he had been in his kitchen on Sparks Street, he told the reporters not to worry—those boys knew what they were doing.

Thinking back on that blithe affirmation thirty-nine years later, I wonder why Brad was so confident in us. He had had little firsthand idea of just how competent we really were, and big mountains are always dangerous. It seems to me now that he was identifying with us. In the same situation as we, high on the Wickersham Wall—as he had proved on Mount Lucania way back in 1937—Brad himself would not have worried, so sure was he of his own talent and resourcefulness.

From that first expedition onward, during the next thirteen years, as I returned to the northern ranges every summer, Brad served as my Alaska mentor. He gave me carte blanche to install myself in the back closet of his top-floor sanctum of an office at the Museum of Science and browse to my heart's content through his thousands of Alaskan images. It was in those vivid, exquisitely sharp photos of faces and ridges seldom seen from the ground that I discovered the routes of my most difficult expeditions, to Mounts Deborah, Huntington, and Dickey. Always Brad offered his candid appraisal of a route I had set my hopes on. Not once did he say, "I think that's too hard [or too dangerous] to try."

On those climbs, we carried Brad's photos to help us with route finding. The prints were so sharp that we could recog-

nize features—a fin of rock here, a curling lip of snow there—
that were as small as two or three feet in width on the ground.
On Mount Dickey in 1974, my two companions and I climbed
the last thousand feet of the 5,000-foot southeast wall in all-
out blizzard. It could have been a matter of life or death to
keep to our planned route, for on the summit ridge two weeks
earlier we had planted a cache, complete with tent, sleeping
bags, and food, which we now absolutely needed to find.

Yet in the whiteout, able barely to see a hundred feet, we
had to admit that everything looked the same—a relentless
50-degree incline of ice and snow seamed with outcroppings
of black schist. Leading our rope of three, I kept pulling a
crumpled Washburn photo out of my parka pocket and scru-
tinizing its details. Thanks to that picture, we hit the summit
ridge within fifty yards of our cache.

Even after I stopped climbing hard, I cherished my protégé-
mentor relationship with Brad. Once I had started writing for
a living, I turned Brad into a subject, publishing three articles
about various aspects of his life and work. And in 1991, he
and I collaborated on a large-format picture book, called
Mount McKinley: The Conquest of Denali, in which a detailed history of deeds on the great mountain served as a platform for a lavish portfolio of Brad's magnificent photos of
North America's highest peak.

Bob Bates never became as close a friend of mine as Brad
did, but I felt in a sense that I knew the man even before I
came to Harvard. The year after Lucania, Bates co-led the
first American expedition to K2, the second-highest mountain
in the world. The team made a gallant attempt, reaching
nearly 26,000 feet before turning back. Then, in 1953, at the

age of forty-two, Bates again co-led a K2 expedition, which ended tragically in the death of Art Gilkey, who was first crippled by thrombophlebitis and then swept away in an avalanche as his teammates desperately tried to haul him down the mountain.

Still in high school, I had read *K2: The Savage Mountain,* the now classic account of the 1953 expedition that Bates co-authored with Charles Houston. The book told such a gripping story that certain scenes were etched for good in my memory. As boys my age kept Willie Mays's over-the-shoulder catch in the 1954 World Series blazed on their eyelids, a touchstone of immortality, so I saw Pete Schoening's "miracle belay," when with one ice axe and brute tenacity he stopped the intertwined falls of six teammates who would otherwise have plunged to their deaths.

Meeting Bates for the first time in the early 1960s, I expected a larger-than-life hero, only to be struck by the self-effacing modesty that anchored the man's character. The limelight only made him uncomfortable: he conveyed the hearty zest for life, oblivious to fame or recognition, that had driven him to decades of expeditioneering. Unlike Brad, who turned his back on serious climbing after 1951, Bob kept it up well into his fifties. In 1985, at the age of seventy-four, Bob participated in an arduous overland expedition to Ulugh Muztagh, an all-but-unknown peak on the border of Tibet and Xinjiang Uygur in China.

In 1994, Bob published a memoir of his life as a climber, traveler, and teacher, called *The Love of Mountains Is Best.* Not a true autobiography, the book is as modest as its author, unfolding in chapter after chapter of old-fashioned adventure yarns. In our modern era of climbers as sponsored athletes, of intensely rivalrous national expeditions to Everest and K2, of film and book deals firmed up long before the team reaches base camp, Bob's narrative has a wonderfully anachronistic quality.

Since I had first learned about Brad and Bob's Lucania expedition, sometime in the 1960s, I had realized what an extraordinary saga their 1937 journey promised in the telling. Yet oddly enough, neither man had published an account of the trip that did it justice. Only a month after the two men had returned to New England, *Life* magazine had come out with an eight-page story about Lucania that handsomely showcased the great photos Brad had managed to bring back. The next year, Brad's understated article about the expedition led off the 1938 *American Alpine Journal,* the journal of record of our mountaineering fraternity. Fifty-six years later, Bob had devoted a characteristically unassuming chapter of *The Love of Mountains Is Best* to the adventure.

About five years ago, Brad started talking to me about how he wished to do a book about Lucania. I concurred at once, hoping my enthusiasm would spur him to a valedictory effort. In the back of my mind, however, I nursed a qualm: that both Bob and Brad had gone at life with such unrelenting optimism, had applied such classically American can-do savvy to everything they undertook, that the true dramatic curve of the story of their greatest exploit ran the risk of being subsumed beneath a kind of aw-shucks panache.

It would take, I thought, a third-person observer to do justice to Lucania—a mountaineer thoroughly familiar with Alaska and the Yukon, who knew just how far "out there"

Brad and Bob had been that dangerous summer, and a writer who need run no risk of immodesty in bringing to light each brilliant or gutsy deed in that tightrope trek through uncertainty. Brad himself wanted me to tackle the story, and Bob warmed to the project. The result is the collaboration embodied in this book.

I harbored, I must confess, a secret agenda. At an even younger age than Brad and Bob on Lucania, my best friend, Don Jensen, and I (we were both twenty) had undergone our own two-man ordeal in the subarctic, a forty-two-day failure on the east ridge of Mount Deborah in Alaska's Hayes Range, culminating in Don's sixty-foot fall into a crevasse from which it took half a day to extricate him. That expedition had unfolded as a slowly gathering nightmare, a trial by frustration and distrust. In the miasma of cabin fever our tiny tent produced, I got so edgy that the very sound of Don's breathing or chewing could drive me crazy. Leery of my impatience, Don retreated into a cocoon of placid silence whose inertia verged on the moribund. The grim journey together nearly cost us our friendship.

I felt it my duty, as I set to work on the Lucania story, to dig beneath the surface of the interpersonal, to find out just what quarrels and tensions and unspoken doubts must have laced Brad and Bob's experience on an expedition considerably more perilous than an attempt on Mount Deborah. The two men's characters, for starters, were so utterly unlike: Brad the headstrong leader, the salty-tongued arbiter of style, quick to anger and unsparing of folly; Bob the peace-at-all-costs go-between, the volunteer for all the dirtiest jobs, magnanimous with others and serene in his own soul.

So I set out to pry beneath the blithe surface and discover the "real" truth about Lucania. In the end, however, I discovered something else: that as far as I could tell, Brad and Bob belonged to a different subspecies of human beings from myself and all the fellows my age I had climbed with. To enter Bates and Washburn's Lucania, I had to walk into an unknown land, peopled with beings I had only read about in Icelandic sagas and Greek myths.

O N E

MAROONED

J U S T before noon on June 18, the skies suddenly cleared. In Valdez, a small coastal Alaskan town tucked into a crooked arm of Prince William Sound, Brad Washburn had cooled his heels during the previous week, watching glumly as one day of rain succeeded another. On June 14, a raging southeaster had swept in off the Gulf of Alaska to batter the town. With the storm came a puzzling, unseasonable warmth.

Brad had rented a ramshackle house in Valdez for five dollars a month, as a place to store the team's gear and food, and as a base for photographic flights he hoped to make after the expedition. Russell Dow, a protégé of Brad's who had been a member of his 1933 expedition to Mount Crillon, a 12,726-foot peak in the Fairweather Range, had been hanging out for months in Valdez, preparing the assault on Lucania.

The other two team members, Bob Bates and Norman Bright, had arrived on board a ship out of Seattle only at 6:00 P.M. the evening before. When June 18 dawned overcast once more, the four men lounged near the wharf, settling in for the indeterminate wait that routinely stalls the fondest plans of aviators in the great North. They were getting ready to eat lunch when the clouds abruptly peeled away, baring a startling expanse of blue stretching from the hills at the town's back to the steely waters of the fjord before it.

Cigarette dangling from his lips, wearing dungarees, a flannel shirt, and a black rain hat, Bob Reeve came storming out of his house and told the boys to forget about lunch and load up the plane for the first flight in. Bob and Brad guzzled down an ice cream soda each and headed for the mud flats below Reeve's house.

Thirty-five years old that summer of 1937, Reeve was one of the three or four finest bush pilots in the Alaska Territory, a paragon among a legendary fraternity of flyers, a good portion of whom would die in crashes in the remote wilderness. Born in a sleepy Wisconsin town, Reeve was afflicted with a congenital restlessness. He had left home at fifteen and talked his way into the Navy shortly after the United States had entered World War I. In 1926, after dropping out of college, he fetched up in Beaumont, Texas, where a pair of barnstormers with the absurdly appropriate names of Maverick and Hazard taught him to fly—the dream of his life since the age of eight, when he had first read about the Wright brothers.

Two years later, Reeve was in South America, flying mail along the roadless wastes of the Andean spine. There was no more perilous aviation being pursued anywhere in the world. One of Reeve's colleagues was Antoine de Saint-Exupéry, who would memorialize the exploits of the South American pilots in *Night Flight*. Reeve learned his craft by trial and error, in the process setting records for the fastest flight between Santiago and Lima and for the most hours flying mail by any aviator in the world in 1930.

The next year, Reeve bumped into a pair of miners from Alaska who enthralled him with tales of "hills full of gold" in the Wrangell Mountains. In South America, Reeve had earned and squandered a small fortune. Now, in the summer of 1932, with the Depression in full swing, he arrived in Valdez as a stowaway on a freighter, hiding under a tarpaulin.

By the next winter, Reeve owned his first airplane—a used Fairchild 51 he bought in Fairbanks. Most of his work came flying freight for miners, whose wildcat prospecting in the Chugach and Wrangell hills bespoke a desperate gamble to escape the poverty that had gripped the nation.

Intensely competitive, fiercely proud of his skill in the air, Reeve had become by 1937 a chain-smoking aerial entrepreneur whose locutions were sprinkled with many a vivid profanity. Tall, thin, ruggedly handsome, with a sourdough's squint, he had gained considerable fame from a number of daring flying feats. Reeve's sense of humor veered between the merely ribald and the downright morbid. Over the door of the small wooden shack that served as his office, he had painted a skull and crossbones, the hand-lettered aperçu, "Opportunity makes damned rascals out of all of us. But opportunity is *not* knocking here," and the injunction, "HANDS OFF OUR TOOLS." The side of the shack bore a curious advertisement for himself: "Always Use Reeve Airways. Slow, Unreliable, Unfair, and Crooked. Scared and Unlicensed [sic]. And Nuts!" The beat-up Model A he drove around Valdez's few dirt streets bore the emblem "Official Car."

Reeve was something of a mechanical genius, attentitively servicing and tinkering with his own planes. Yet paradoxically, he was at the same time a throwback, a seat-of-the-pants aviator. He never learned to fly on instruments, and long after radios became virtually mandatory for pilots in Alaska, Reeve refused to carry one.

Brad Washburn recalls a characteristic Reeve anecdote from World War II, when the pilot had finally capitulated and succumbed to radio contact. "He was flying freight down the Aleutian chain, to build up the anti-Japanese bases. Although his plane couldn't carry big loads like some of the others, Bob always got through. One day he was coming into Umnak, a god-forsaken place. He got on the radio and said, 'Reeve—Umnak.' Umnak radioed back, 'For God's sake, Bob, don't land here, it's pouring, it's zero-zero [visibility and ceiling], and it's blowing like hell.' Bob answered, 'I'm already on the runway. I'm trying to find you, for Christ's sake.'"

As a pilot, Reeve was also a great innovator, which was the reason Brad had sought him out for Lucania. Following the lead of aviators in the Alps, a few Alaskan pilots had begun to experiment with wooden skis instead of wheels, for winter and glacier flying. Reeve soon cornered the lucrative market flying supplies into mines in the Chugach and Wrangell Mountains, landing on skis at improvised strips near the high diggings. Once spring had melted the snow in Valdez, however, Reeve had to cease his supply flights because he could no longer land in Valdez on skis.

It was the innovator's notion that, with the right kind of skis, he might use the coastal mud flats below Valdez's gravel strip for takeoffs and landings during the warm months. Wooden skis would only rot if left to sit in the tidal muck. So Reeve commandeered a stainless steel bar from a derelict roadhouse and cobbled out of it a pair of metal sheaths to fit over the wooden skis. Then he practiced on the mud flats until he had mastered the slithery game. Because he could land and take off only at low tide, the pilot now carried a tide table with him wherever he went. But now he could haul freight into the Chugach and Wrangell mines year-round.

By the winter of 1936–1937, Brad, only twenty-six years old, was already the veteran of four expeditions to Alaska and the Yukon. Setting his sights on Lucania, the highest unclimbed mountain in North America, but a dauntingly remote objective, Brad conceived of the idea of flying in to make a landing high on the Walsh Glacier, just south of the sprawling mountain, thereby obviating a grueling approach march through the foothills.

Brad had heard about Reeve's virtuoso mud-flats work. In January 1937, the climber wrote the pilot. He outlined his plan for Lucania, then added (a trifle condescendingly), "Although I've never met you, I know several of your best friends who believe that you are exactly the fellow who we need to do all of the flying that will be required to assure the success of this little expedition. . . . We believe that you are plenty experienced to handle this work—and that if we succeed on Lucania, you are certain to get a lot of favorable publicity—both for you as well as for the town of Valdez. We hope that you'll agree to be our pilot."

Reeve wired back a one-sentence answer: "ANYWHERE YOU'LL RIDE, I'LL FLY."

Just after 1:00 P.M. on June 18, Reeve, Washburn, and Bates loaded up the Fairchild 51. Normally, after high tide had receded, "Mudville," as the strip was dubbed, was a slimy miasma into which an intruder sank ankle-deep, but now, with a fierce sun fast drying out the flats, Reeve asked his charges to slosh down the runway in front of his plane. If the flats baked dry, taking off was impossible. Brad later recorded the six-hundred-foot takeoff in his diary: "We just barely made it, our skis just clearing the ditch and tall eel grass at the end of the runway. The plane wobbled a bit; Bob nosed her level to pick up speed, and in a moment we were banking gently out across the bay, climbing toward Thompson Pass. Bob turned around and grinned his wonderful grin from underneath that inseparable rain hat."

Already, in May, Reeve had made three landings with Russ Dow on the Walsh Glacier, laying a depot of 2,000 pounds of gear and food in preparation for base camp. On the first flight, Reeve had turned back in the face of violent winds, but on his second try, he had glided to a perfect landing at 8,750 feet. Here, where winter still reigned, the snow was as hard as concrete. Reeve's landing was the highest yet made in Alaska or Canada, and the highest ski-equipped landing anywhere in the world with a full load of freight.

In May, the logistics had been altogether different. Reeve had ferried the team's gear in several flights from Valdez to McCarthy, a gold-rush town in the Wrangell Mountains where, in late spring, there was still plenty of snow on the ground. Then, with Dow in the passenger seat, he had made the three trips back and forth from McCarthy to the Walsh Glacier.

Now, on June 18, the snow had melted off the McCarthy strip. Reeve had no choice but to take the climbers in on a single round trip from Valdez. Yet such a flight—more than two hundred miles each way in a direct line—was beyond the fuel capacity of his craft. Thus among the baggage the three men had loaded aboard the Fairchild were five-gallon gas cans carrying enough fuel to ensure Reeve's return. This gambit in turn required that he land *somewhere,* for once beyond his half-tank turnaround point, the pilot would be forced to put down and refuel. With all Reeve's mechanical savvy, he had not figured out any way to pour gas into the plane's tank while it was still in the air.

Still, given the ease of the May landings and the perfect weather, Reeve was confident as he took off. He would fly Bob and Brad and their personal gear in on the first flight, then return for Russ Dow and Norman Bright, flying them and the rest of the team's equipment in that same day, if the weather held. Perhaps a month later, after they had climbed Lucania, Reeve would fly the men out by pairs.

Bob and Brad, in turn, had full confidence in their pilot. As Brad recalls, "Reeve could land on a peanut." After only thirty minutes in the air, as the Fairchild sped east against a stiff headwind toward the great Copper River, the men saw the first high cirrus clouds and layers of altostratus materializing on the horizon. At 2:45, they passed over McCarthy, the last outpost of civilization. Now Reeve headed up the gorge of the Chitina River, to cover the last eighty air miles before he would land on the Walsh Glacier. His passengers gazed somewhat apprehensively out either window at the terrain beneath them. "The Chitina River is huge and muddy," wrote Brad later in his diary; "it swings in countless meanders back and forth across its wide, flat-floored valley. On each side rugged rocky mountains walled it in."

Twelve years before, arduously relaying depots of supplies, the team that would make the first ascent of Mount Logan had trudged up this difficult gorge. Otherwise, it lay virtually unexplored. It was obvious to the three men in the Fairchild that the Chitina offered not the ghost of a hope of an emergency landing strip.

The weather was growing steadily worse. "Cumulus clouds hung in pennants behind the peaks," wrote Brad later. The head of the Chitina Valley was swallowed in a solid gray wall of mist and fog.

Since he had taken off, Reeve had chain-smoked one cigarette after another. Now his anxiety grew manifest. Sixty-four years later, Brad would recall another tribulation about that flight. "Reeve had worked out a way that he could pee past the stick and out a hole in the floor. The whole damn plane smelled of dried piss." To add to the discomfort, the flight was a bitterly cold one for the passengers in the back seat, since to aid Brad's aerial photography Reeve had taken the right-hand door off the plane.

The Fairchild passed over the snout of the Chitina Glacier and headed up its massive ice stream. Now Reeve beckoned to Brad to lean forward for a consultation. Shouting over the engine, the pilot said, "That cloud bank ahead is too low. We have ten minutes more before we'll have too little gas to get home. What do you think?"

"Anywhere you'll fly, we'll ride," Brad answered.

Yet in his diary the following night, Brad recaptured the savagery of the landscape the men flew over during the next fifteen minutes. "Till my dying day I shall never forget that nauseating desolation of dying masses of ice. . . . The valley walls on both sides were vertical rock and scree, bare, snow-less, and bleak. Potholes full of horrid muddy water filled every depression in the hellish sea of stagnant ice."

At 3:40 P.M., well past the turnaround point, the plane reached the lower stretches of the Walsh Glacier. With the eye of a prospector, Reeve gestured toward a hillside off the left wing that looked to him as if it probably bore ore. "Anybody can have that gold mine who wants it!" he shouted.

The Walsh looked as forbidding as the Chitina. "The ground below," Brad would write, "was still a chaos of filthy, rotten ice and twisted moraines, gutted and criss-crossed with crevasses." Concurring with Brad's unspoken judgment, Reeve called out, "Hell's asshole, ain't it?" Then: "We'll make it!"

The Fairchild was flying at 9,000 feet. Only a few hundred feet above, a "leaden ceiling of clouds," in Brad's phrase, cut off the visible world. The turbulence was extreme, as the small craft bounced and veered against the headwind.

Just after 4:00 P.M., Reeve shouted, "There she is!" Brad and Bob peered at the white sweep of the glacier ahead, until they too spotted the tiny black dot of the cache Reeve and Dow had established in May. "We're going to land, boys. Hold on!"

Reeve cut the engine; the rigging hummed as the plane plummeted toward the snow. Landing in flat light on a featureless glacier is one of the toughest tasks in bush flying. By 1937, pilots had already learned the trick of making a preliminary pass while throwing out a series of dark objects—gunny sacks dyed black, willow boughs—that, lined up where they came to rest on the glacier, gave depth to the illusory perspective. Such a gambit was now a luxury that Reeve could not afford.

At the last minute, Reeve pulled back on the stick. The plane touched down with a feathery swish. Reeve gunned the engine so the Fairchild could hop over a crevasse that suddenly appeared. In a surprisingly short distance, the plane slowed to a stop. Reeve let the motor die. It was 4:07 P.M.

Brad hopped out the right door of the plane, and sank thigh-deep into a sea of slush.

IN his four years of glacier landings, Bob Reeve had never seen the like. During all the seasons Brad and Bob would climb in Alaska, they would never again encounter conditions remotely similar to these. The week of freakish warmth before June 18 had softened up the surface of the Walsh Glacier, which had been so conveniently firm for Reeve's landings in May. And day after day of rain, at an altitude where in a normal summer only snow fell, had turned the glacier to soup.

Reeve had come in for the landing at a spot where he calculated his decelerating glide would leave an easy taxi up to the gear cache. Instead, the slush had gripped the Fairchild like wet cement. The plane had come to rest, slumped almost belly-deep in snow, a full three-quarters of a mile below the cache.

The pilot instantly grasped the implications. On such a surface, it would be a very hard job to get up enough speed to take off.

As part of his emergency gear, Reeve carried a pair of snowshoes in the Fairchild. Brad strapped these on and started off toward the cache, hoping to retrieve two more pairs of snowshoes and a pair of long bamboo tent poles with which to probe for crevasses. Although he was in prime shape, Brad had spent the winter at sea level: now, floundering in the soggy snow, gasping in the rarefied air at 8,750 feet, he needed twenty-five minutes to cover that three-quarters of a mile. The solo dash was dangerous, too, for he had no idea whether serious crevasses lay athwart his path. (These monstrous cracks, formed by the strain of a glacier's imperciptible flow downvalley, often form as relatively narrow slits on the surface that bulge to considerable widths twenty or fifty or a hundred feet down. If the crevasse opening shows on the surface, it is a straightforward matter to skirt it. But often the winds drift snow across the slit, gluing a treacherous bridge across the aperture that completely camouflages the gulf beneath. Many an experienced mountaineer has died falling, either roped or unroped, into a hidden crevasse. Traveling unroped on an unknown glacier, as Brad now was forced to do, is usually considered the height of recklessness.)

There were indeed crevasses. "Very gingerly and scared stiff," wrote Brad, "I approached [the gear depot] by a series of wide zigzags." The cached snowshoes, as luck would have it, lay near the bottom of the pile; Brad had to pull aside four or five hundred pounds of boxes to retrieve them.

Meanwhile, at the Fairchild, as soon as Brad had headed off toward the cache, Reeve had said to Bates, "Let's get 'er gassed up right away." The two men poured the contents of the five-gallon gas cans they had hauled to the Walsh into the tank.

Then Reeve said, "See if you can dig 'er out. I'll try to taxi up to Brad." With manic energy, Bob used Reeve's shovel to dig away at the submerged skis, clearing a ramp just in front of the plane. Reeve got back into the cockpit and fired the engine. As Bob recalls, "He rocked the plane to get the skis loose. Then he started uphill, with me running along behind him in the deep snow." Heading back toward his teammates with the extra snowshoes, Brad beheld a disheartening scene. "I watched the plane coming toward me up the gentle grade," he wrote the next evening in his diary, "wallowing and roaring in the slush. Then, all of a sudden, the left wing slumped toward the snow, stopping only a yard from the ground. The motor roared louder, and then the wing sank to within a foot of the surface. From where I was, it appeared to be *on* it."

The trio made a second try, with Bob and Brad taking turns digging out the now more deeply submerged craft. It took forty minutes of nonstop toil before Reeve was ready. He gunned the engine and rocked the plane, while Brad and Bob yanked on a rope tied to its tail; at last the Fairchild lurched out of its glacial hole. This time Reeve managed to taxi the plane several thousand feet up-glacier before it slumped once more. Recognizing defeat, at the last moment Reeve turned the plane sideways, so that it sat parked at right angles to the slope. Brad and Bob snowshoed up to the plane; then Reeve jacked it up so they could put wooden blocks under the skis to prevent the craft's freezing in during the night. "Quite a work-out on an ice cream soda apiece!" wrote Brad in his diary.

The only option was to wait for night and hope the temperature plummeted low enough so that the glacier might firm up. At the moment, however, the thermometer read 40°F, at an altitude where 20 to 25°F would have been normal in July. To make matters worse, rain squalls began to sweep the Walsh.

The three men trudged up to the cache, arriving exhausted at 7:00 P.M. Bob and Brad dug out the big four-man Logan tent and pitched it; then they rooted through the gear for sleeping bags and air mattresses. Even puttering about camp was perilous. Wrote Brad, "Both Bob and I fell into small cre-vasses not ten feet from the tent but caught ourselves with the shovel. . . . The whole place is just riddled with crevasses."

In Bob's memory, "We were so tired from gassing up the plane and digging it out, we didn't feel like eating very much. We cooked up some soup and crackers and ate a little cheese."

Reeve was known for his fiery temper: the townsfolk of Valdez talked about several legendary brawls in which he had taken part. But according to Bob, in the face of this unprece-dented setback on the Walsh, Reeve neither ranted nor cursed, but maintained a stony silence: "He looked pretty gloomy when we got to the cache." Still, all three protagonists felt confident that in the chill of early morning, Reeve would be able to take off on a newly frozen runway. As the men fell asleep around 10:00 P.M., it was still raining.

During the night, the temperature dropped no lower than

39°F. The men woke to find the slush that surrounded them unconsolidated. Attempting a takeoff was out of the question. Reeve stayed in the tent all day. A warm sun burned through banks of clouds; at noon, the thermometer read an outrageous 55°F. Trying to put a brave face on things, Brad and Bob roped up and snowshoed a mile or two up the glacier, reconnoitering the route they had set their hearts on six months before. At their high point, the clouds cleared for a few minutes, giving the men their first glimpse of the summit of Lucania, capped by a lenticular bonnet, towering 8,000 feet above them.

Reeve's funk deepened. The pilot was, Bates later wrote, "wild to get home." It was not as though he had never before been forced to sit by his stranded plane and wait out the weather. In February 1933, flying a couple, their four-year-old son, and their four-month-old baby to Nome, Reeve ran into a whiteout and had to make a forced landing on the frozen bed of the Kateel River. Hauling logs to build a bonfire, the pilot kept his passengers alive through a twenty-five-hour ice fog that prohibited takeoff; in the night, the thermometer reached minus 55°F. It was for this survival feat that Reeve first made newspaper headlines.

Several years later, alone in his Fairchild, Reeve ran into a violent storm and had to put down on a high divide only fifty miles from Valdez. There he waited out five days of bad weather, camping in his cockpit, living on canned corned beef and Ry-Krisp, using his tools to tune up the plane while he killed the empty hours.

In 1935, however, Reeve had met a spunky young woman named Janice Morisette, who hailed from a small Wisconsin town not far from the pilot's birthplace. As restless of spirit as Reeve himself, Morisette had read about the aviator's exploits and got up the nerve to write him a letter, asking, "Do you need a secretary, bookkeeper, or extra mine hand?" After a four-month correspondence, Morisette announced her imminent arrival in Valdez. The confirmed bachelor, terrified of women, fled on a prospecting trip to Canada rather than greet his pen pal. But curiosity modulated into romance. In 1936, the couple married.

Morisette's first job in Alaska was as secretary to the Road Commission in Valdez. As Reeve later told his biographer, Beth Day, "Punching that ole typewriter, with her black hair and all, she reminded me of Tillie the Toiler." "Tillie" Miss Morisette thus became, in homage to the famous comic book character of the '20s and '30s, a beautiful flapper turned hardworking stenographer. In early 1937, she gave birth to the couple's first child, Richard.

Thus as Reeve loitered, trapped by slush on the Walsh Glacier through June 18 and 19, he badly missed his wife and his infant son—and worried about their worrying about him. Had the flight been routine, Reeve should have landed back in Valdez by 7:30 or 8:00 P.M. on the 18th. Twenty-four hours later, with no sign of him, "Tillie"—and Russ Dow and Norman Bright—could have only feared the worst: a crash landing, possibly a fatal one. No other pilot in or around Valdez had enough knowledge of the terrain to go check on Reeve. The Fairchild carried no radio, and in any event, no receiving station on the ground could have heard his distress call had he broadcast one.

If too many days passed and Reeve failed to appear, the

bush pilots of Alaska would launch an all-out search, for despite their internecine rivalries, they looked after their own. In November 1929, when the most famous of them all, Carl Ben Eielson, disappeared on a bold attempt to push a flying route from Alaska to Siberia, all the best pilots in the territory launched a heroic search, despite the grim conditions of an Arctic winter. It took more than two months, however, before a pair of them found the wreckage of Eielson's plane on an obscure hillside near the Siberian coast.

In the evening of June 19, as further token of the fluky weather, a violent thunderstorm crossed the glacier (such tempests are rare at 9,000 feet in Canada). Though the storm brought another deluge of rain, by 10:00 P.M. the temperature had dropped to 33°F, giving the men hope for an overnight freezing.

The rain, however, persisted through the night. Discouraged, the men lolled in their bags until 11:00 A.M. on June 20. In mid-afternoon, Brad decided to dig a pit to see how deep the snow lay here at 8,750 feet. Only six feet down, he hit bare ice. Both he and Bob had assumed that far more snow had accumulated over the long winter. Evidently, the rain and warmth had washed away months' worth of drifts.

This new discovery added to the men's sense of alarm, for it made it likely that, a month hence, those scant six feet of cover would have melted off, leaving bare ice and open crevasses, an impossible surface for a ski-equipped plane to land on. At the end of the expedition, Reeve would thus most likely be unable to return to pick up the team. They would have to hike out from the Walsh Glacier.

At this point, however, Brad and Bob were still thinking in

terms of a four-man team. On June 20, in a letter to his parents that he hoped Reeve might carry out with him, Brad expressed his first doubts about that fact: "Bob [Reeve] won't be able to get in after the first of July so we must walk out. . . . In fact, I think we'll be lucky if we can get the other two boys in here before the snow is getting too thin for safe landing. Bob and I are going to make a very careful search for cracks after Bob Reeve leaves for Valdez, and mark out with flags a safe runway for his next landing."

Meanwhile, in the tent, Reeve brooded on, keeping his silence, gazing often at a photo of Tillie he carried with him. Hoping to improve his morale, the two climbers urged Reeve to join them for a roped stroll up-glacier, but the pilot refused. "You skin your skunks and I'll skin mine," was his gruff reply.

"Bob Reeve is so scared of cracks," Brad wrote in his diary on June 20, "that he has not moved an inch from camp!" Washburn was right on this score, but at the time he was ignorant of the immediate cause of Reeve's terror.

Just two years before, in the spring, Reeve had been eating dinner in a Valdez café when a miner stumbled in, hands and feet frozen. The man and his partner had been caught out on the Valdez Glacier just above town in a sudden storm. The partner had been left there, in danger of freezing to death.

Reeve leapt from the table, collared two friends, climbed into his Fairchild, and made a daredevil landing on the moraine beside the Valdez Glacier—terrain on which he had never before attempted to put down. Up on the ice, the trio of rescuers found the miner near death. They wrapped him in their coats, improvised a litter of sorts, and started to haul the victim toward the plane, but before they had gone a mile, the prospector expired. By now it was almost pitch dark. The three men left the body and hurried back to the plane.

In the darkness, Reeve stepped suddenly into empty space. Instinctively, he flung out his hands and caught hold of a rock imbedded in the wall of the crevasse. Before his strength gave out, his friends managed to pull him back to safety. They made their cautious way to the plane and flew back to Valdez. A dog team retrieved the body in the morning.

Twenty years later, Reeve described that near-accident to Beth Day, as she made notes for her biography, *Glacier Pilot*. According to Day, "The shock of that fall is almost as sickeningly vivid to Reeve today as it was then. For years afterward, he had to force himself to walk down an ordinary sidewalk in the dark."

Dinner on June 20 was a bit more "royal" (in Brad's phrase) than it had been the first night on the Walsh. The men cooked Knorr pea soup and then a goulash of chicken, rice, and gravy mix. They washed it all down with a drink made from powdered lemonade. By 8:00 P.M. the temperature was down to 32°F, the coldest yet. "A thin crust is beginning to form," noted Brad in his diary.

Sixty-four years afterward, neither Bob nor Brad can recollect just how their friends Russ Dow and Norman Bright handled the long wait in Valdez without news. Nor did Beth Day think to interview Tillie about the cruelties of that vigil. Every bush pilot's wife in the territory knew that she had to live with the constant fear that each flight might prove her husband's last. Yet Tillie would have also known that the landing on the Walsh was far more dangerous than a routine ferry of supplies to a Chugach mine. And parenthood adds a heavy burden of angst to the bargain anyone who loves an adventurer strikes with fate.

The ordeal of those three—Tillie Reeve, Dow, and Bright—lies, unfortunately, beyond recapturing, for none of them is alive today. Nor is Bob Reeve.

Brad and Bob had jumped into the Fairchild for the first flight simply because they were the more experienced mountaineers. Yet it was by no means inevitable that that pair would have made up the team's vanguard. Sometimes the leader of the party comes in on the last flight, after tidying up the last details of the frantic logistics that always bedevil a mountaineering expedition.

Be that as it may, the luck of the draw now dictated that Dow and Bright would be excluded from a journey that would turn out to be one of the great American adventures of the century. Brad and Bob share a vague sense that their friends took this huge disappointment in stride, that they stayed good sports to the end. Brad had chosen the men for that sort of quality. Neither was a first-rate climber, but Bob Bates himself had had only scanty mountain skills when Brad first met him at Harvard. Throughout his two-decade career of Alaskan campaigns, Brad would again and again choose his partners not for their technical ability, but for their character. What he sought above all was the capacity for hard work, the ability to get along under stress, a sunny zest for an arduous challenge.

Russ Dow had met Brad in early 1933. Dow climbed with Washburn on the Mount Crillon expedition. As Brad remembers, "Russ Dow was just solid gold from the marrow of his bones to the top of his head. He was a hell of a nice guy and a very strong backpacker. He didn't get very far up the mountain, but we depended on his competence, and he was always fun to have around base camp."

In 1937, learning that Dow was unencumbered by career or school, Brad recruited him to form the one-man advance guard for Lucania. Arriving in Valdez in mid-spring with a ton of expedition supplies, Dow took a series of odd jobs while he helped Reeve organize the shuttle to McCarthy, then flew in on the historic May flights to lay the depot on the Walsh.

Norman Bright had a different background. A student at the University of Washington in Seattle, he was introduced to Brad and Bob by a mutual friend. He had done a little climbing, but in 1937, Bright's claim to fame was that he was one of the top track stars in the country, second only to Glenn Cunningham in the two-mile. To accept Brad's invitation to Lucania, he had to turn down a spot on an All-American track team touring Japan that summer.

Bob traveled with Bright by boat from Seattle to Valdez. "He was completely broke," Bob recalls, "so we traveled steerage. We got along wonderfully with the cook and the crew, so they gave us extra of everything. At each little port on the way to Valdez, we would get off and help the stevedores move baggage."

WHEN the three men on the Walsh awakened the morning of June 21, they were seized with wild hope. The freezing had done its trick: the surface of the glacier had turned to crust, atop which lay an inch of fresh snow. At 8:00 A.M., the trio snowshoed down to the plane. Brad gave Reeve the several letters he had written to be mailed from Valdez. Yanking on the tail, the men straightened the plane so it pointed down the runway. The pilot climbed into the cockpit, started the engine, and gunned the plane downhill.

As Bob and Brad watched, their elation turned to despair. After a promising first few hundred yards, the Fairchild began to bounce. Instead of gaining speed, the plane seemed to slow down. Later the men understood what had happened. The crust was only a thin glaze over a still unconsolidated swamp of slush. With each bounce, the plane broke through the crust, plunging deeper into the slush each time. Reeve managed a full mile of lurching, bouncing progress, a parody of a takeoff, before grinding to a halt just uphill from a mass of crevasses.

As fast as they could, Bob and Brad wallowed down the glacier to rejoin their comrade. There was nothing to do but tie a rope to the tail, turn the plane around, and let Reeve try to taxi back to where he had begun his abortive flight. The newly exposed slush proved diabolical. After only a hundred yards, the Fairchild slumped halfway in, up to the wingtip. Bob and Brad hiked all the way back to the cache, retrieved the shovel, and headed down once more to the stranded plane. They dug for half an hour before Reeve tried again. He managed three hundred yards. Now the plane lay more deeply mired than ever: the left wingtip actually was stuck a foot beneath the surface of the snow.

For the first time, Reeve began to wonder whether he might lose his plane altogether. With the energy of desperation, Brad and Bob recommenced their digging. "This time it was a terror of a job," Brad told his diary; "she was in at least six feet deep and at a terrific angle."

It took three full hours of digging, then ten separate savage gunnings of the engine, before Reeve managed to jolt the Fairchild out of its potential grave. Only halfway back up the travesty of a runway, the pilot parked the plane sideways once more; then he jacked the craft up so Brad and Bob could plant wooden blocks under the skis. They returned to camp, oppressed by dark thoughts.

"Bob Reeve is a stoic and a prince," wrote Brad that afternoon. "He certainly took the two wrecks this morning calmly." But Reeve was making his own calculations. Quite apart from the dangerous futility of his failed takeoffs, each attempt used up precious gas. He might well eventually get airborne, only to run out of fuel before reaching Valdez.

By now the three men acknowledged that there would be no second flight. "It is a terrible shame for Russ and Norm," Brad recorded, "but it would be ridiculous to risk their lives and Bob's on another flight in here." He added, "It will be absurd to try to take off again until we have rock-hard crust, even if it means waiting a month."

Now Brad suggested to Reeve an even gloomier option. "Why don't you leave the plane for another time," he proposed, "and walk out with us?" If Reeve answered at all, it was with a scowl.

In one sense, the men faced no immediate danger. There was so much food in the massive cache that they could indeed have waited a month for the Walsh to firm up. But for a man unwilling to take a single unnecessary step outside the haven of the tent, that prospect was unthinkable. So was the gauntlet of a hike out, across those eighty desolate miles of glacier, scree, boulders, alder thickets, and surging brown channels of the Chitina River that they had peered down upon on the flight in.

That night, Reeve's fourth on the glacier, the temperature dropped to 27°F, but a dense fog rolled in. Bob and Brad hiked with their shovel down the makeshift runway, filling holes in the slush, planting gas cans as markers.

The men were up at 3:45 A.M., assessing the conditions. (At 61 degrees north latitude in June, it grows no darker than dusk, and one can climb or work all night.) Fog still shrouded the glacier, but the temperature hovered a few degrees below freezing. Brad went to work over the camp stove. "We cooked all seven of our eggs in one final batch of delicious scrambled eggs," he wrote later, "broke into a fresh package of bacon, had a grand compote of peaches and pears. . . . My secret motive for such a large breakfast was to be well fortified to dig the plane out of another hole should it go in."

Around 6:00 A.M., Reeve started the Fairchild's engine to warm it up. The men returned to camp and waited, while, slowly, patches of blue sky began to puncture the fog. Just after 8:00, they hurried back to the plane.

Reeve had determined to make a last-ditch effort. Now he threw out of the cabin every scrap of gear he could, to lighten the plane—tools, emergency sleeping bag, first-aid equipment, survival food, even the crank for the engine. At the last minute, to Bob and Brad's amazement, he took a ball-peen hammer and started pounding away at the propeller. To the master tinkerer, a sharper-pitched prop would bite better in the thin air, assisting a shorter takeoff at the cost of aerial stability. At the last moment, Bob and Brad scraped the remnants of overnight frost off the plane's wings and tail.

Without so much as a wave good-bye, Reeve started down the glacier. Bob Bates recounts the next few moments: "He went bouncing down the runway. He hit a great block of snow and it bounced him off the left side, where the slope fell off quite steeply toward a meltwater lake on the glacier. Quick as he could, he turned the nose of the plane right for the lake, gave it everything he could. By the time he got to the lake, he had enough speed to get off, just missing the water. He kept going right toward a cliff on the side of the glacier."

Suddenly, the plane vanished beneath a dip in the glacier's surface. Bob and Brad literally held their breath, anticipating the sound of a crash. As Brad later recorded in his diary, "All of a sudden, a few seconds later, the plane came into sight. . . . It was going like fury, but this time she was steady, her right wing lower than her left." The plane climbed, then gathered speed down-valley.

In 1957, Beth Day documented what the escape had felt like from the pilot's seat: "I gave it the gun," said Reeve, "and off I went. But, by God, I hadn't gone a hundred feet when smack! down into a crevasse. But I wasn't stopping. . . . I climbed right out of the crevasse and kept going. Then flop! down into another—and I lost the air speed I'd gained, getting out of it. Bumpety bump, it was just like driving over a plowed road. I realized I was getting nowhere. I'd already run a mile or more, and ahead of me I could see the big crevasses—wide enough to hold a boxcar. If I hit them, I was a goner. Then I happened to glance left, and spotted an icefall, shearing off the side— maybe 250 feet drop. It was my last chance. I made a sharp left turn and dove the plane right over that icefall. . . . The plane had achieved just enough speed on the jump-over to become airborne. I leveled out about ten feet from the bottom.

"That was the greatest feeling of my life—bar none!"

Later Reeve told Brad that when he arrived in Valdez, he "would gladly have thrown a lighted match into the fuel tank," it was so empty.

As the Fairchild dwindled in the distance, Brad and Bob screamed with relief and joy. Then they sat down in the snow, beside the boxes that for the moment held all their worldly possessions, and tried to catch their breath. The plane vanished behind Lucania's western spur, and soon they could no longer hear its fading whine.

An immemorial silence reclaimed the mountains. In that moment, the gravity of their situation came home to these best of friends. Brad and Bob were marooned in the heart of the Saint Elias Range, eighty miles by air from the nearest prospector at McCarthy, at least 120 miles by the route they would have to pursue to escape. No one else—not even the bravest pilot in the territory—could help them now. They were on their own.

T w o

FAST AND LIGHT

I N some ways, it was an unlikely meeting. Bob Bates and Brad Washburn had gone through their freshman year at Harvard without bumping into each other. Now, at the beginning of their sophomore year, in September 1930, Bob lived in Dunster House, while Brad was lodged in Lowell House—only two blocks apart in the streets of Cambridge, but fairly distinct realms, socially speaking.

Brad was already a minor celebrity within the highly competitive ranks of Harvard. Three years before, at the age of seventeen, he had published a book called *Among the Alps with Bradford*. One in a series, "Boys' Books by Boys," cooked up by the flamboyant publisher George P. Putnam, who would soon become the husband of Amelia Earhart, Brad's slender account of his teenage climbs with famous guides out of Chamonix was so popular that it came out in a number of foreign editions, including one in Hungarian.

Thanks to this renown, Bob recognized Brad by sight when he saw him crossing Harvard Yard, but he was far too modest a person to force an introduction. That task fell to Walt Everett, a climber who knew Brad through Lowell House and who had gone to Phillips Exeter Academy in New Hampshire with Bob. Washburn, who had gone off on his first Alaskan expedition the previous summer, was looking for candidates to staff future ventures. One day Everett said to Washburn, "Hey, I've got an interesting friend whom you would really enjoy. He lives over in Dunster House." Everett proposed inviting Bates to dinner in Lowell House, but cautioned, "The guy has never climbed. He doesn't know anything about climbing. I don't know if he's ever had snowshoes on. But he's just a hell of a nice guy."

Inexperienced though he was, Bates shared with Washburn a love of the White Mountains in New Hampshire. That autumn of 1930, Everett, Bates, and Washburn made weekend excursions to the Presidential Range. Bates and Everett took turns riding in the rumble seat of Brad's Model A Ford, which he had bought with his earnings from *Among the Alps with Bradford*. Brad had named the roadster Niobe, not out of some deep classical erudition, but because, driving to the Whites, the trio invariably passed through the center of Sandwich, New Hampshire, where a statue of the tragic figure from Greek mythology crowned the town hill. (Zeus turned Niobe to stone as punishment for boasting of the beauty of her children, whom Apollo and Artemis slew.)

Brad decided that his new friend ought to join the Harvard

Mountaineering Club. The only problem was, Bates was underqualified. Henry Hall, who had founded the club six years earlier, had stipulated that membership be granted only to alpinists who had climbed "three major glacier-hung peaks or their equivalent"—a requirement not coincidentally tailored to Hall's favorite range, the Canadian Rockies. Though only in his early thirties, Hall had already become something of an *éminence grise*, and he was not about to loosen the rules just because Bob Bates was "a hell of a nice guy." After much squabbling, Washburn managed to invent a special category of associate membership for the likes of Bates. Thus the man who would become one of the foremost American mountaineers of the century slipped, at nineteen, through the back door of an undergraduate club that was already in danger of becoming a bastion of climbing conservatism.

The next fall, with his entrepreneurial flair, Brad persuaded the Forest Service to let the HMC build a cabin on Mount Washington, just below Tuckerman Ravine, which, in a time before chairlifts, was the favorite ski area in New England. The new Fire Trail, really little better than a broad hiking path, led past the proposed site. To haul building materials, Brad coaxed Niobe up the trail. "We had two big rolls of that horrible roofing paper," Brad recalls, "each one of which weighed ninety pounds. Nobody wanted to carry the damned things, so we put them in the back of Niobe and drove right up the trail. Got within a quarter mile of the cabin site. The only way to get the car turned around was to back it into the woods; then everybody lifted it around. Everybody was yelling and screaming and drunk with beer. We just had a marvelous time."

As much as anything, the communal effort of building the cabin welded the students into a mountaineering brotherhood to be reckoned with. And there, in the White Mountains, Brad's partnership with Bob was forged.

Bob had grown up in Philadelphia, where he was born on January 14, 1911. His father was a professor of Greek and classical archaeology at the University of Pennsylvania. An enthusiasm for things Roman and Hellenic rubbed off on the impressionable youngster. When Bob published his autobiographical memoir in 1994, he chose his title from a little-known inscription. In 1558, a Swiss adventurer had climbed an easy peak in the Alps, only to find that some predecessor had carved in Greek on the summit rock a motto that translated as "The love of mountains is best."

Bob claimed he was first imbued with this feeling at the age of five, when his family hiked to the top of Flying Mountain, which towers a lordly 284 feet above sea level on Mount Desert Island off the coast of Maine. The small boy was entranced by granite ledges, ripe blueberries, the smell of the sea breeze mixed with the scent of fern and spruce.

Four years later, Bob nearly died in the great influenza epidemic of 1919. The passage in his memoir detailing his escape from that untimely end bespeaks the character that would carry him toward Lucania eighteen years later:

> I became very ill and would not eat. Apparently, I was considered unlikely to survive until one evening my brother came to my bedroom with a piece of chicken from the dinner table and ordered me to eat it. I did, and from then on I improved. I have rarely been ill since.

The Bateses spent several summers in a rented cabin on Randolph Hill in New Hampshire, which looked across a valley toward Mounts Adams and Madison, two of the highest summits in the Presidential Range. Bob spent every day in the woods, conducting wood-chip races in a nearby brook, exploring trails fraught (or so he thought) with the possibility of running into bears. His most vivid memory of those youthful days in the White Mountains comes from the first night he was allowed to sleep in a mountain hut, on Madison. In the middle of the night, Bob was awakened by terrible screams.

A German professor, or a professor who taught German, I never knew which, had gone to the outhouse in the dark, where he made contact with a porcupine who was chewing the seat. Whether the professor actually sat on the porcupine we were never sure, but I always speculated that he had.

Two cardinal encounters during his childhood promised to deepen Bates's fascination with mountains. He came across a classic mountaineering book, *Scrambles Amongst the Alps,* by Edward Whymper. The climactic chapter in that book tells the canonic saga of the first ascent of the Matterhorn in 1865, when Whymper saw his joy turn to ashes as, on the descent, four of his six teammates fell to their deaths. (Despite that tragedy, more climbers of Bates's generation were nudged toward mountaineering by Whymper's work than by all other climbing books combined.)

The other encounter would also, in retrospect, have a monitory as well as an inspirational impact. In 1923, when Bob was twelve, he attended a lecture at the University of Pennsylvania Museum. The speaker was George Leigh Mallory, unhappily touring the States as he tried to raise money for the 1924 Everest expedition. "Pretty dangerous, I thought, but exciting, too," was the twelve-year-old's reaction.

A year later, the loss of Mallory and Irvine confirmed my impression of the dangers of climbing the world's biggest mountains, but as succeeding years brought new expeditions, my father and I read about them eagerly. Of course, I had no thought of ever taking part in such efforts.

During the summer between Exeter Academy and Harvard, Bob and a friend spent two weeks on a whirlwind driving tour of Maine and eastern Canada. They climbed Mount Katahdin, the most "serious" peak in the eastern United States, after a sleepless night during which a torrential rainstorm soaked them through their sleeping bags.

Nonetheless, by the time he arrived at Harvard, Bates had done no real mountaineering. During his freshman year, when he decided to major in English, Bob buckled down to his studies as he had not in secondary school. In the summer of 1930, while Brad was off attempting a major unclimbed peak in Alaska, Bob and a classmate made an aimless and disappointing car-camping trip through the Midwest. The pretty girl whom Bob's pal hoped to track down proved elusive, the road by which the vagabonds planned to circumnavigate Lake Superior turned out not to exist, and their Peerless automobile broke down with dismal regularity.

When he was nineteen, then, it was by no means inevitable that the love of mountains would prove to be the central thread of Bob Bates's life. The same cannot be said of Brad Washburn. Half a year older than his friend, Brad was born in Boston on June 7, 1910. His father was dean of the Episcopal Theological School in Cambridge. An avid outdoorsman, Henry Bradford Washburn, Sr., took his two sons—Brad and Sherry (Sherwood), who was a year and a half younger—on frequent excursions to the White Mountains.

At eleven, Brad made his first ascent of Mount Washington. Like Bates, Washburn was plagued with a youthful illness. "As a child, I suffered terribly from hay fever," Brad told Anthony Decaneas in an interview in the late 1990s. "In 1921, when I first climbed Mount Washington, I realized that my hay fever disappeared at higher altitudes. Climbing and hiking became a relief from hay fever."

At fifteen, with Sherry and his father, Brad made his first winter ascent of New England's highest mountain. So keen was his passion for the White Mountains that by the age of sixteen, he had written a guidebook, *Trails and Peaks of the Presidential Range*, which was privately published by Brad's uncle. That same year, on his family's first visit to the Alps, he reached the summits of three of its giants, Mont Blanc, Monte Rosa, and the Matterhorn. The first two were strenuous "walk-ups," but the last was still a significant climb, sixty-one years after Whymper's disastrous first ascent.

The next summer, during a two-month stay in Chamonix, Brad and Sherry hired the celebrated guides Alfred Couttet, Georges Charlet, and Antoine Ravanel and became true alpinists, learning their craft as seconds on the rope on such redoubtable granite spires as the Grands Charmoz and the Grépon. "Georges said that Sherry and I were the first clients he'd climbed with who were eager to be criticized," Brad would recall seventy-three years later. "He said that most of his clients didn't want to be told what to do. But we wanted to know if we did something wrong or stupid, so that we wouldn't do it again. We wanted to climb better."

Sherry would never climb again after 1929—an ex-mountaineer at age seventeen! He would go on to a distinguished career at the University of California at Berkeley, becoming one of the top physical anthropologists in the world (well before it became the accepted view, he argued that the Piltdown man was a hoax). "Sherry was better on rock than I was," Brad reminisces. "Georges used to say about him, 'Il grimpe comme un chat' ['He climbs like a cat']."

Two years earlier, George P. Putnam had launched his "Boys' Books by Boys" series with *David Goes Voyaging*—an account of a three-month journey in the Pacific with the naturalist William Beebe, written by Putnam's own twelve-year-old son. Two further *David* books were followed by *Deric in Mesa Verde* and *Deric with the Indians,* penned by the then thirteen-year-old son of Jesse Nusbaum, the cranky superintendent of Mesa Verde National Park.

It was only natural that, learning of Brad's exploits from an article about his Matterhorn climb that Brad had contributed to *Youth's Companion* magazine, Putnam would sign him up for a book. (Brad eventually wrote three, following up *Among the Alps with Bradford* with *Bradford on Mount Washington* and *Bradford on Mount Fairweather,* the last authored at age twenty, when he hardly qualified as a "boy.") Of the first book, Brad recalls, "I wrote it in ten days at the Pensione Calcina in Venice, on the way back from

Europe. Turned in the manuscript to Putnam, as agreed, on the fifteenth of September, with a batch of pictures. The book was on sale by November, pictures interleaved in the right places in the text. Can you imagine a publisher doing that today?"

Along with his passion for climbing, those teenage summers in the Alps inculcated in Washburn twin fascinations with flight and photography. Before he had caught more than a distant glimpse of the mountains, he flew in a small plane out of Lyon with his father one July day in 1926 on a sightseeing junket. That first tour of the Mont Blanc massif by air informs the rapturous first chapter of *Among the Alps*.

As a Christmas present in 1925, Brad was given a Kodak Vest Pocket Autographic camera—ironically, the same model that disappeared with Mallory on Mount Everest. Brad's mother gave him a crucial piece of advice. "She told me I should take pictures of people *doing* things—not just scenics," says Washburn. The excellent photographs Putnam published in *Among the Alps* indeed show people doing things: Sherry in black beret jumping a crevasse, Brad seconding Charlet on the vertical rock of the famous Mummery Crack on the Grépon (camera evidently handed over to Sherry for the shot), five happy friends lounging on the boulders before the refuge of the Grands Mulets.

While Bob Bates was attending Exeter Academy, Brad was enrolled in the Groton School in Massachusetts, another exclusive private secondary school. There, one day in 1926, the sixteen-year-old climber sat spellbound as Captain John Noel showed his photographs from the 1924 Everest expedition, recounting the experience of waiting in vain at Camp III for Mallory and Sandy Irvine to return, then, when all hope was gone, retreating in disarray to base camp on the Rongbuk Glacier, where the survivors built a memorial to their lost comrades. Noel's lecture instilled in Brad a lifelong fascination with Everest, which came to fruition sixty-two years later, when he published the definitive map of the world's highest mountain.

Summers in Chamonix, Groton, his own Model A roadster . . . It sounds as though Brad was born with the proverbial silver spoon in his mouth. But as he went off to Harvard in the fall of 1929, the stock market crashed, ushering in the Great Depression. Washburn's parents could not afford to pay the full Harvard tuition, so Brad put himself through school on bank loans, on the proceeds from his Putnam books, and by going on lecture tours, precociously passing himself off as a kind of junior Lowell Thomas, an eighteen-year-old authority on adventure.

Among the Alps with Bradford is a blithely written, almost cocky *récit* of two young acolytes having the time of their lives in the mountains. Despite the fact that Brad was only seventeen when he wrote it, the book gives insights into the character of the man who would become the foremost Alaskan mountaineer and explorer of the century.

On their first major excursion on the Aiguille du Midi, a startlingly sharp pinnacle that looms 7,000 feet above Chamonix, Brad and Sherry worked out a way to reassure their anxious mother that everything was okay. At dusk, from the porch of the hut at the Plan de l'Aiguille, the boys prepared a Roman candle and a "red fire, with which to signal mother in the valley."

When the appointed time arrived, Sherry ran out onto the terrace of the rocks below our window and touched off the red fire, while I fired off the Roman candle from the window.

A moment later we saw a light blinking furiously from the window of the hotel [in Chamonix], far below us. We replied with a few flashes made by passing a hat before our candle.

In the midst of climbs, there were carefree diversions unthinkable today:

We had some canned pineapples, and when they were finished I amused myself by throwing the can over the cliff, and listening to it as it dropped and dropped, banging and clattering over the rocks for nearly a minute, before it was lost to sight and sound in the distance.

On hard pitches in the 1920s, guides routinely hauled their clients up like sacks of potatoes. The brothers Washburn, however, were determined to second the pitches under their own steam, changing from hobnailed boots to sneakers (which "stuck like glue," Brad claimed) for the tricky bits of rock climbing. In a charming introduction to the book, Sherry bragged about his older brother:

You can hire a guide who will pull you up any difficult places there happen to be on a mountain, but Brad usually gets up by himself. He agrees with those who believe that mountain climbing is a test of sportsmanship, and feels that if he can't climb the difficult places without being pulled he really hasn't climbed the mountain.

Setting out for an August 1927 assault on Mont Blanc, at 15,771 feet the highest peak in western Europe, immediately after a heavy snowstorm, Brad and Sherry hired a porter as well as the guide Georges Charlet. There is a hint of the pampered rich kid in Brad's rationale for doing so: "It's always necessary to have a porter on that climb because it's so long and fatiguing for anyone under twenty-five years old, that it is good to go without anything on your back at all."

In the end, a second fierce storm defeated the party. Sherry turned back early, though Brad pushed to the top of the Col du Dôme, only two hours in good weather from the summit. Guide, porter, and client alike suffered minor frostbite. The closing passage of *Among the Alps,* voicing Brad's sanguine acceptance of the setback, uncannily anticipates the decision he and Bob Bates would face on Mount Lucania a decade later:

> There's nothing like the game in which you match yourself against Nature. Give her your very best and fight to the end, but when you see that she has got the upper hand, turn, and don't be scared to admit defeat. It's the fool who sticks to it when it's impossible. . . . [A]fter all, there's nothing like the feeling of knowing that you've done your best, even though you've lost in the struggle!

In 1929, between Groton and Harvard, Brad spent one last summer climbing in the Alps. By then, he was an accomplished mountaineer. No longer a mere client, but a near-equal partner to his celebrated guides, Washburn that season went after unclimbed routes. His crowning deed was the first ascent of the north face of the Aiguille Verte with Georges Charlet and Alfred Couttet—the boldest climb yet done in the Chamonix area, still regarded more than seven decades later as a watershed in Alpine climbing. To be sure, Couttet and Charlet led most of the pitches, but at nineteen Brad pulled his own weight.

Looking back on that accomplishment in the year 2000, Brad recalled the vaulting ambition that drove him to the Verte. "Sherry had gone back home, and I was staying in France for a couple of extra weeks. Couttet was one of the finest climbers in the Alps, and he thought that the two best unclimbed routes around Chamonix were the north face of the Aiguille Verte and the Walker Spur on the north face of the Grandes Jorasses. So Alfred went over to the hut beneath the Walker and spent a couple of days sitting there looking at the face with his field glasses. I paid him ten bucks a day to do it. He came back and said, 'I don't like it. There's too much rock fall.' Remember, in those days we didn't have helmets. So we did the north face of the Verte instead."

The Walker Spur would defeat a number of daring attempts before falling to a team led by the formidable Italian climber Ricardo Cassin in 1938. By that year, it was common to refer alternately to the Walker or to the treacherous north face of the Eiger in Switzerland (solved the same summer, only after eight of the first ten aspirants were killed trying) as "the last great problem" of the Alps. To think of assaulting the Walker in 1929, as Brad had, was to be far ahead of one's time.

Entering Harvard, then, Washburn had good reason to regard himself as the equal of any mountaineer his age in the country. That freshman year, however, Brad saw his geographical priorities radically reoriented. Presiding over the HMC was Henry Hall, with his years of experience in the Canadian Rockies and his participation in the remarkable 1925 first ascent of Mount Logan in the Yukon, the second-highest peak in North America and, in terms of sheer bulk, the largest mountain in the world. At one HMC meeting, Brad listened enthralled as a somewhat senior explorer, W. Osgood Field, spoke of his journeys among the fjords and peaks of Alaska's Glacier Bay. Then, at an American Alpine Club meeting in New York, Brad met Allen Carpé.

A research engineer at Bell Telephone Labs and a student of cosmic rays (which are best detected at high altitudes), Carpé was probably the most outstanding expeditionary climber of his day in America. He had been a driving force on the Mount Logan ascent. In 1926, he had made an attempt on 15,292-foot Mount Fairweather, a beautiful, isolated giant of a mountain looming over Glacier Bay in southeast Alaska.

Compared to the crowded Alps, Alaska promised limitless wilderness and challenges at every hand. "I was just fascinated," Brad says today of these glimmerings from the North. "This was a new place. Very few people had been there."

A less confident mountaineer (or for that matter, one with the temperament of Bob Bates rather than Brad Washburn) might, at nineteen, have sought to become a protégé of Allen Carpé, hoping to be invited along on the next attempt on Fairweather, which Carpé had called in print "now perhaps the outstanding unclimbed mountain in America." Instead,

Brad boldly organized his own Fairweather expedition for the summer of 1930. Having just turned twenty, Brad landed his team by boat at Lituya Bay and set out to knock off Fairweather.

The attempt ended in abject failure. Brad's party wore themselves out relaying loads twenty-four miles from Lituya Bay to the foot of the great mountain. At the end of their probe, the men had reached the paltry altitude of 6,700 feet— some 8,600 feet short of the summit.

Thus rather than becoming Carpé's protégé, Washburn became his rival. Spurred to action, Carpé returned to Fairweather in 1931, with, as teammates, three of the strongest expeditionary climbers in America. Moving with a logistical efficiency that had eluded Washburn, Carpé's quartet planted a series of camps up the south face of the mountain. Finally, on June 8, Carpé and Terris Moore stood on the summit of Fairweather.

Moore barely knew Washburn by 1931, but they would become close friends for life. In later years, Moore told Brad about the decision, while the quartet was marooned in a high camp during a storm, to send the other two climbers down. "Terry said that they were running low on food, and finally Carpé said, 'We've got to divide this party up because we haven't got enough food for all of us to get to the top.' So he and Terry stayed in camp, and [the other two] went back down. Terry told me that the last thing Carpé said, as the group broke up, was, 'If we don't climb this goddamned mountain now, that son of a bitch Washburn will come back and do it next year.'

"'Cantankerous Carp,' everybody called him. Carpé

scared the hell out of Terry. He didn't like climbing roped; he felt the rope was a damned nuisance. Nobody ever said Carpé was not a hell of a good climber, but high on the shoulder of Fairweather, he slipped and barely avoided falling to his death. Climbing unroped, of course, eventually cost Carpé his life." The very next year, Carpé and Theodore Koven, skiing unroped on the Muldrow Glacier on Mount McKinley, fell (probably simultaneously) into a huge hidden crevasse. The site of the unwitnessed accident was discovered two days later by another party descending the mountain. Koven lay dead, face-down, on the glacial surface, having apparently summoned the effort to struggle out of the crevasse before he succumbed to his injuries and the cold. Carpé's body was never found.

By the time Brad began cavorting in the playground of Europe (to use Sir Leslie Stephen's felicitous epithet), climbing in the Alps had a glorious history of 140 years, stretching back to the first ascent of Mont Blanc in 1786. The last major summit to be climbed was the Matterhorn, by Whymper, whose ill-starred ascent in 1865 closed what was even then called the golden age of mountaineering.

In contrast, by the time Brad landed at Lituya Bay in 1930, alpinism in Alaska was barely forty-four years old. The three highest summits in Alaska and the Yukon had been reached, but all of the technically most difficult peaks—the Matterhorns of the North—were still virgin. Whole ranges lay unexplored, even unnamed.

The initial lodestone for mountaineering in the North American subarctic was Mount Saint Elias, a graceful peak that thrusts to the improbable altitude of 18,008 feet only twenty miles from the Gulf of Alaska. Sighting the mountain on July 20, 1741, while still 120 miles from land, the Russian explorer Vitus Bering made the European discovery of Alaska.

For nearly two decades after 1880, Saint Elias was thought to be the highest peak on the continent (it is actually fourth, after McKinley, Logan, and the Mexican volcano Orizaba). The first two attempts to climb it, in 1886 and 1888, got nowhere. In 1890 and 1891, a pair of expeditions sponsored by the National Geographic Society and the U.S. Geological Survey, led by a redoubtable geologist named Israel Russell, made a real dent in the mountain's defenses. On the second venture, Russell and two companions struggled to reach a high col that would prove to be the key to the first ascent.

That came only in 1897, at the hands of a lavishly equipped team led by Luigi Amedeo di Savoia, the Duke of the Abruzzi. At the time of his birth in Madrid, Luigi, though Italian, was son of the ruling king of Spain. After his father's death in 1890, the king of Italy bestowed on the seventeen-year-old the title of Duke of the Abruzzi—a post that required precious few official duties. In the shambles that was Italian politics in his day, the duke might well have slipped into a life of luxury and dilettantism. Instead, he became one of the greatest mountaineers and explorers of his era.

As he sailed for America in May 1897, Luigi Amedeo was only twenty-four, but he had under his belt not only ten years of solid service in his country's naval schools, but an enviable record of hard climbs in the Alps, including a new route on the Grandes Jorasses. Having pondered the failures of his predecessors on Saint Elias, the duke, in the words of his cobiographers, Mirella Tenderini and Michael Shandrick, "decided to plan his expedition as if he were going to the North Pole instead of climbing a mountain."

From Italy, he brought five companions and four professional mountain guides. In Seattle, he hired an American outfitter who recruited ten porters to haul loads from the seacoast to base camp. On disembarking at Yakutat Bay, the party unloaded the mind-boggling quantity of 6,600 pounds of food alone.

In logistical style, the expedition was a curious blend of the modern and the old-fashioned. The team's spiffy Mummery tents weighed only three and a half pounds each, but the duke had also brought ten iron bedsteads so that he and his well-born compatriots need not suffer the indignity of sleeping in direct contact with the ground. (In the end, five of the bedsteads were hauled by the porters fifty-five miles from the beach to advance base camp. The guides were content to rough it, bedsteadless.)

With those guides tackling the technical passages, by July 30 all ten Italians had reached the high pass below the summit on the north, which the duke named Russell Col, in honor of the geologist who had paved the way there in 1891. The next day, all ten men made it to the summit, though on top they were so exhausted that the duke himself had to undertake the meteorological observations he had assigned to his colleagues.

In terms of the legacy this first great Alaskan ascent bequeathed to Washburn and Bates, there would be three intriguing linkages. Twelve years after Saint Elias, the duke led an expedition to K2, the world's second-highest mountain. On that mountain in 1909, he reached the extraordinary altitude of 24,275 feet—the highest anyone had ever been on earth to that date. In so doing, the duke pioneered the route (called today the Abruzzi Ridge) by which Bob Bates's 1938 team would reach a new high on the mountain, turning back a mere 2,000 feet below the top. K2 would not be successfully climbed until 1954, by a strong Italian party.

One of the duke's teammates on both Saint Elias and K2 was Vittorio Sella, universally acclaimed as the finest mountain photographer in history—before Bradford Washburn, that is, with whom he now must share that accolade. Struggling against impossible conditions to expose large-format photographs with his heavy and temperamental cameras, then to develop the pictures on the spot in a black tent brought along for that purpose, Sella lost many of his best images to such unexpected mishaps as condensation from his own breath gathering on the gelatin paper he used. So determined, however, was Sella to get good summit pictures, that he reclimbed the mountain the following day with a different camera.

When Washburn turned his passion toward aerial mountain photography in the late 1930s, Sella's by then famous pictures set an Olympian standard toward which the young American strived. Though he never met Sella, the Italian became a model for Brad. A touchstone was Sella's dictum— "Big scenery should be photographed with big negatives." The crystalline clarity of Brad's own best pictures, shot with frozen fingers out of the open doors of planes bouncing in the turbulence, owes much to Brad's choice of a series of heavy Fairchild cameras that expose eight-by-ten-inch negatives.

The third linkage had to do with the view the ten Italians had from the summit of Mount Saint Elias. Thirty-five miles away in the northeast, the whole horizon seemed to be taken up by the sprawling bulk of Mount Logan. But off Logan's left shoulder, twice as far away, loomed another giant peak. On the spot, the Duke of the Abruzzi named this second mountain Lucania, after the name of the ship on which the expedition had sailed from Liverpool to New York. The Italians were not the first nonnatives to see Lucania: prospectors in the Yukon lowlands had doubtless caught sight of it looming over nearer, lower mountains. But the Italians were the first to put its existence on official record.

In 1897, the same year that Saint Elias was climbed, a gold miner named William A. Dickey wrote a now-famous letter to the *New York Sun*. Dickey had spent the previous summer in the Alaskan interior, panning on the Susitna and Chulitna Rivers. Impressed by the huge glaciated mountain hulking to the north on clear days, Dickey performed a crude survey of its summit, and came up with the surprisingly accurate estimate of 20,000 feet for its altitude (the mountain is now known to rise 20,320 feet above sea level).

Dickey claimed that the "new" mountain might be the highest on the continent. And he suggested a name for it. The first news his party of sourdoughs had received on emerging from the wilderness the previous summer was of the nomination of William McKinley for the presidency. A staunch Republican, Dickey slapped on the mountain that was indeed the highest in North America a name that could not have been more inappropriate—for the twenty-fifth president not only never traveled anywhere near Alaska, he seems to have been singularly uninterested in the territory.

The "original" name for the mountain, Denali, which has come back into vogue during the last two decades, is only one of a number of appellations by which the indigenous Indians referred to the peak. "Denali" means "the high one" or "the great one." The careless legend has come down to us that Dickey was the (nonnative) discoverer of Mount McKinley, but this would be preposterous. Not only had many miners and trappers come relatively close to the mountain by 1897, but on a clear day, McKinley is plainly visible from Cook Inlet, 150 miles to the south. From their ships, not only Captain George Vancouver in 1794, but Captain James Cook and any number of Russian mariners before that had almost certainly seen the peak.

Lying so far inland as it does, McKinley poses greater logistical problems of approach than does Saint Elias. The first two "attempts" on the mountain, in 1898, were really only reconnaissances of its lowland defenses. Depending on what one calls a genuine attempt, McKinley would repel some eleven expeditions between 1898 and its relatively clockwork first ascent in 1913, by a party led by the forty-nine-year-old Hudson Stuck, archdeacon of the Yukon.

By all odds the most bizarre and remarkable of these attempts was the work of a team of gold miners in 1910, who, completely untrained in mountain climbing, decided to drop their prospecting for a few months and pull off an ascent that "professionals" and "outsiders" seemed incapable of. By 1909, McKinley had become the talk of the camp at the Kantishna diggings, north of the mountain—particularly the acrimonious disputes over Dr. Frederick A. Cook's claim to have reached the summit with one partner (a virtually mute Montana horsepacker) in 1906. (In later life, having become an assiduous student of North America's most audacious exploration hoax, Brad would debunk Cook's claim beyond the shadow of a doubt. Yet in 2003, legions of true believers in the doctor's absurd boast still abound.)

The catalyst for what would come to be known as the Sourdough Expedition was a $5,000 saloon bet that McKinley would see a first ascent by July 4, 1910. Hoping to get rich from the wager rather than from the endless toil for gold, four prospectors worked their way up the northeast side of the mountain through the spring of 1910, unerringly pioneering the route by which Stuck would succeed three years later. By March 18, three of them had established a high camp at 10,900 feet.

On April 1, they set out with the bold intention of climbing the last 9,400 feet in one day. So fit were they, so undaunted by crevasses or potential avalanche slopes, that they might well have succeeded, but for an odd yet understandable decision.

McKinley has two summits: the true south summit, at 20,320 feet, and the north summit, at 19,470 feet. Despite the 850-foot difference in their altitudes, it is almost impossible to gauge from the upper Muldrow Glacier which is higher. (Because it is nearer, indeed, the north summit can look higher.) The Sourdoughs chose the north summit, however, mainly because it could be seen from Fairbanks. As if climbing more than 9,000 feet at high altitude in a single day were not challenge enough, the trio took turns lugging a fourteen-foot spruce pole which they planned to plant near the summit, flying a flag from it so that the skeptical might see their marker by telescope from the Kantishna gold diggings about forty miles to the north.

Two of the three, Billy Taylor and Pete Anderson, reached the north summit at 3:25 P.M., in temperatures of minus 30°F, shortly after erecting their flagpole on a prominent spur just below the top. Alas, the spruce tree was far too small to be spotted from Fairbanks, even with the best telescopes. Taylor and Anderson returned to the diggings to find their claim of victory dismissed as roundly as had been Dr. Cook's. Vindication came in 1913, however, when a sharp-eyed member of Stuck's party saw the pole with the naked eye from a plateau 2,000 feet below it and two miles away.

After the first ascent of the Matterhorn in 1865, climbing in the Alps continued at a fever pitch. Whether or not the so-called golden age had ended, alpinists were driven to push the limits by putting up new routes on peaks that had seen only a handful of ascents.

The same was not true of Alaska. After the first ascent of McKinley, climbers turned their back on the Far North for a dozen years. The campaign that ended that neglect, ironically, was born in emulation of the British Everest expeditions of 1921, 1922, and 1924.

By 1925, the first- and third-highest peaks in the North had been claimed; but the second-highest, the gigantic massif of Mount Logan (19,550 feet, only 770 feet lower than McKinley) had not even been reconnoitered. Only the ambitious Boundary Commission party of 1913, which probed the lower reaches of the glaciers flowing west from Logan, had called attention to Logan's promise as an objective, though the commission's report labeled the terrain a land of "utter desolation."

The summit of Saint Elias forms the pivotal corner of the border between Alaska and Canada. McKinley, of course, lies in the interior of Alaska. But Logan is a wholly Canadian mountain, sprawling in its seldom-seen obscurity at the heart of the Saint Elias Range, its summit a good twenty miles east of the border. Thus its conquest became an obsession of the Alpine Club of Canada.

Thinking in terms of a North American Everest, expedition leader Albert MacCarthy decided to lay a series of caches along the arduous 140-mile approach route. To do so, he started work in the bitter cold of February. Launching his campaign from McCarthy, the same gold-rush town from which, twelve years later, Russell Dow and Bob Reeve would fly in the ton of supplies for base camp on Mount Lucania, MacCarthy and five teammates used two horse-drawn sleds and three dog teams to get a considerably larger pile of food and gear distributed in depots along the Chitina River gorge. Temperatures ranged as low as minus 45°F. Harnesses on the horses froze so badly, they could sometimes not be removed for two weeks straight.

After two months of fiendishly hard work, the long string of caches was in place. In May, MacCarthy led the team of eight men toward the mountain. By June 22, six climbers were still in the hunt, having pitched a camp on the summit plateau, above 18,000 feet.

The most dangerous aspect of a Logan climb is not any stretch of particular technical difficulty, but the sheer size of that summit plateau, unparalleled elsewhere on earth. The problems range from trying to guess which of several peaks is the true summit, to getting lost in a storm, to spending too much time exposed in high winds at altitude. All of these hazards now afflicted MacCarthy's team, despite their fanatically thorough preparation. The peak they thought the summit lay two miles from the actual highest point; the extra four miles of trudging in the thin air seriously overextended the party. On the descent, the two ropes of three got separated from one another in a whiteout, and the weaker trio got disoriented by a full 180 degrees, so that the men started to follow their own willow wand markers back toward the summit. All six men survived an open bivouac at 19,000 feet, with a temperature of minus 12°F. By the time the party reached the lower slopes, all the men were utterly played out.

It was only good luck that kept the Logan ascent from costing the lives of several of its members. Yet the triumph was widely hailed as a brilliant success. The British *Alpine Journal* editorialized, "Greater hardships have probably never been experienced in any mountaineering expedition." A measure of the team's achievement lay in the fact that on Logan, unlike Saint Elias and McKinley, the first party to attempt the mountain reached the summit.

Only four years later, as Bates and Washburn arrived at Harvard, the mentor-in-residence was Henry Hall, a veteran of the Logan climb (though one of the two men who did not make the summit). With membership in the HMC, which Hall had founded, came the implicit doctrine that the Logan style—a massive buildup of relayed loads and caches, months in the approach, heavy camps fortified for long stays—was the way to attack the remote prizes of Alaska and the Yukon. That doctrine, however, Brad and Bob would do their best to demolish.

Not all at once, however. Washburn's 1930 failure on Mount Fairweather had rubbed his nose in the sheer enormousness of the logistical challenge on an Alaskan snow-and-ice giant. Rather than return to the North, Brad spent the next summer in Chamonix, not tackling virgin routes but helping a friend, Burton Holmes, make a film of the standard route up Mont Blanc. It would be one of only three summers in a stretch of sixteen consecutive years during which Brad did no significant mountaineering.

Recalls Bob Bates, "Brad asked me to go on Mont Blanc with him in 1931, but I didn't have any money." During their sophomore year, the "hell of a nice guy" in Dunster House and the boys' adventure writer over in Lowell had spent a lot of time in the White Mountains together. A week or two after he returned from the Alps, Brad talked Bob into trying to break the speed record for the hike from Pinkham Notch to the top of Mount Washington. The record—4,000 feet of ascent in one hour and twenty minutes—was held by the crusty caretaker of the Pinkham Notch hut, Joe Dodge.

"I was tough as nails from climbing in the Alps all summer," Brad recalls, "but poor Bob had been lobster fishing in Maine. He sort of died out on Lion's Head."

A passage in Bates's memoir, *The Love of Mountains Is Best,* dovetails with Brad's recollection. "I stayed with Brad to the top of the [Tuckerman] headwall, which we reached in an hour, then sat down and waved him on. I didn't stay long, however, and was only a few minutes behind when he reached the summit."

"Never did break Joe Dodge's record," Brad adds. "We did it in an hour thirty."

Throughout the school year, Bob and Brad went off nearly every weekend on HMC climbing or skiing trips. Though their style of mountaineering would prove to be prophetic in the great ranges, in one respect the two twenty-year-olds were already reactionaries. Figures associated with the HMC only a few years before—notably Ken Henderson and Robert Underhill—had brought the techniques of the Alps to New England, where they pioneered daring rock routes on such cliffs as Cannon Mountain and Cathedral Ledge.

The HMC climbers of Bob and Brad's era, on the other hand, were uninterested in rock climbing. There were no afternoon outings to Quincy Quarries, no Saturday sessions at Joe English or Crow Hill, where later generations of HMCers would perfect their rock technique. To this day Brad brags of having driven only one piton in his life.

This might seem puzzling, given Brad's virtuosic apprenticeship on the Chamonix aiguilles. At an early age, however, Brad recognized that rock work would play very little part in the first ascents of the remote and glaciated mountains of the North that would become his life's mission. The HMC's weekend training on ice, on the other hand, was at a high level. In chopping steps up the 70-degree incline of blue ice in Pinnacle Gully on Mount Washington, Brad would perform a climb that was still considered an achievement thirty years later. In 1980, one of the central figures in that HMC gang, H. Adams Carter, who for thirty-five years single-handedly edited *The American Alpine Journal,* insisted, "Don't let anybody tell you that Brad wasn't damned good technically. I would say that technically Brad was the best [in our circle]."

By the summer of 1932, Brad was headed for Alaska once

more. His objective was Mount Crillon, at 12,726 feet, more than 2,500 feet lower than Fairweather (which lies twenty-five miles to its northwest) but in every other respect an equal challenge. This time Bob Bates was a member of the team.

It would take Brad three successive summers and three expeditions to knock off this pesky mountain. The first year, 1932, his team exhausted its resources simply sorting out the unknown geography that lay between Lituya Bay and the base of the mountain. By the end of the trip, the climbers had reached only the initial cliffs on Crillon, but from that low vantage point, they saw what looked like a good climbing route.

The next year, with Bob once more on Brad's team—both men having graduated from Harvard just a few weeks before—the party took advantage of its hard-earned knowledge from 1932. On July 29, in a blowing mist, Bob, Brad, and Walt Everett (the friend who had introduced the two to each other three years before) struggled up a steep ice pitch to stand on what they were sure was Crillon's summit. The barometer actually read 254 feet higher than the mountain's known elevation. The men shook hands and congratulated each other.

In the next moment, one of the cruelest tricks that fate can play on mountaineers unfolded with its heartless logic. As Bob would write in *The Love of Mountains Is Best,*

> Brad tied the American flag to a trail marker and was taking a picture when Walt asked, "What peak is that?" Clouds kept blocking the view, but we could glimpse a peak ahead. At first we thought it was Fairweather, but in a few minutes

we had a better view. It was the summit of Crillon and still a long way off. We were on the high point of the ridge, but not on the summit.

With no time left to push on, the 1933 expedition thus saw victory slip through its fingers.

Nothing if not dogged, Brad put together another team in 1934, and at last reached Crillon's summit with two companions. Bob was not one of them, however, despite being invited on the expedition. Pursuing an M.A. in English at Harvard, with an offer of a instructorship at the University of Pennsylvania for the following autumn, Bates felt duty-bound to spend his summer in the library (where he pored over the works of the eccentric antiquarian and biographer John Aubrey) rather than on an Alaskan glacier. Asked sixty-seven years later whether it had been painful to miss out on Crillon's ascent after two summers' trying, Bob was philosophical: "No. I made my choice. I wished Brad luck, and I was glad when they climbed it."

Throughout his life, Brad Washburn has been the sort of man who does not readily accept defeat. Brad's first three Alaskan expeditions, strictly speaking, were failures. With success on Crillon in 1934, however, he began a string of eighteen years in the mountains that utterly reversed that discouraging initial course.

On Fairweather and Crillon, Brad and his cronies evolved the style that would revolutionize big-range mountaineering in North America. Step by step, they rejected the logistical overkill embodied in the 1925 Mount Logan expedition, in favor of a streamlined approach to penetrating remote regions. Though their gear and food were not markedly superior to their predecessors', Brad and Bob in the early 1930s learned to move fast and light.

Curiously, more than six decades later, the two men have a hard time articulating the reforms that went into their fast-and-light style. So thoroughly have their ideas gained the day, it is as though they cannot recall an era in which things were done differently in the mountains.

Today, Bob and Brad point to their food-bag system: on Crillon, one day's food for six men was stuffed into each of several identical bags, so that a person knew exactly how many ration units he had loaded into his pack. That principle by itself, however, hardly explains the HMC teams' new efficiency.

As early as 1932, Brad had taken advantage of the airplane to approach Alaskan mountains. For three years running, he had landed by floatplane at Lituya Bay, rather than approach by boat. In 1934, he gave the party a huge boost by arranging airdrops of supplies at base camp (the first time this gambit had been employed in the North), and he succeeded in using intercamp VHF radios on the mountain.

The core of the fast-and-light style, however, must be seen as a matter of nerve and daring. The earlier expeditions, overwhelmed by the scale of the northern wilderness, hedged against risk by making sure there were always ample stores of food, gear, and tents to which to retreat in an emergency. The HMCers under Brad, on the other hand, began to feel that they could do without some of those safety nets. Above all, they came to feel utterly at home on high ridges and crevassed glaciers, as even the Duke of the Abruzzi had not in 1897. (It is significant that in more than twenty years of campaigning in Alaska and the Yukon, not one of Brad's HMC circle would ever suffer serious frostbite.)

At the same time in England, two farsighted Everest veterans, Eric Shipton and H. W. (Bill) Tilman, were comparably reforming Himalayan climbing, turning their backs on expeditions equipped with tons of gear and hundreds of porters in order to prosecute bold forays into blank regions on the map with a colleague or two and a couple of porters. These legendary climbers, who would eventually become friends with the HMCers, made their own independent discovery of "fast and light" in the remote ranges.

After graduating from Harvard in 1933 (Brad cum laude in French history and literature), both men stayed on for graduate study. Bob earned his M.A. in English the summer that he devoted to John Aubrey instead of to the mountains. Brad started graduate work in the Harvard Institute for Geographical Exploration, a quirky but cutting-edge facility that has long since ceased to exist.

At this point, but for a few twists of fortune, the close friends of four years' standing might have begun to drift apart. In September 1934, Bob arrived at the University of Pennsylvania, ready to begin the life of an English instructor, only to receive a rude shock. The embarrassed dean told him that far fewer students had enrolled at Penn than anticipated. The job Bob had been promised had evaporated.

Deeply disheartened, Bob started taking courses toward a Ph.D., and accepted a stopgap job "practice teaching" at the secondary school he had attended before Exeter. A phone call in late November suddenly interrupted the desultory course of his career.

That same autumn Brad had written an article about Mount Crillon for *National Geographic,* commencing a life-long association with the society in Washington, D.C. It had not taken the young adventurer long to sweet-talk the NGS into a wonderful boondoggle.

In his memoir, Bob recalls the first words Brad spoke into the telephone from Cambridge to Philadelphia. "Bob," said Brad, "the National Geographic Society wants us to map those mountains we saw [from Crillon] north of Mount Saint Elias. We'll leave after Christmas and travel on the glaciers with dog teams. They'll pay all expenses. Can you come?"

Bob's reaction was instant:

> Could I come? . . . If I had had a job teaching, I couldn't have done it, but I was free—free to help chart the last large blank space on the map of North America! I was ecstatic. All I had to do before departure was to write papers for the courses I was taking. There were no final exams.

It was characteristic of Brad's *noblesse oblige* that he phrased the mandate as "the National Geographic Society wants us" to chart the blank on the map. Ever since staring at the frozen wilderness from the south, Brad had had his heart set on exploring it.

Just how unknown that blank region was can be gleaned from a perusal of the map Brad's party carried into the field in early 1935 (see photo insert). The document, zealously guarded by Brad through more than six decades since the expedition, has the look of an ancient chart found in some obscure archive. The burn marks on its edges were inflicted on the Lowell Glacier (named by the party), when a tent collapsed onto the camp stove, incinerating Brad's sleeping bag, several articles of clothing, and the tent itself, and nearly consuming the team's only map. Brad sketched on the map in pencil his own approximations in the field of the gigantic glaciers his party discovered and was the first to explore. Mount Lucania appears in the upper left corner, its southern approaches charted by the Boundary Commission in 1913, but all the terrain north and east of it virtually featureless.

What was officially titled the National Geographic Society Yukon Expedition remains to this day one of the most ambitious exploratory jaunts ever undertaken in the North. The whole scheme was Brad's, but among the party he recruited were two men whose expertise stretched into areas Brad himself knew little about. Andy Taylor, then in his early sixties, was a longtime prospector who had come to the Klondike in 1898 and stayed on, perfecting the various arts of overland travel in the subarctic. Though not trained as a mountaineer, Taylor had been probably the steadiest member of the 1925 Mount Logan party. Johnny Haydon, born on Kluane Lake to an English father and an Indian mother, was an expert dog musher.

Only Brad might have concocted an expedition that would marry state-of-the-art bush flying with dogsled teams. Rather than enter the wilderness by creeping toward it from the edges, Brad planned to fly in to establish a base camp in the very heart of the region.

That blank space comprised 6,400 square miles of glaciers and mountains. Not only, as far as anyone knew, had no human beings, native or otherwise, ever traversed it; by 1935 no pilot had had the nerve or incentive to fly over it. The excellent flyer Brad recruited, Bob Randall, was constantly apprehensive while airborne over that frozen wasteland. As he told Bob Bates of the region where Brad proposed to set up base camp, "If we have to make a landing out west of the Alsek [River], I might as well just nose her straight down; it would be much more simple."

In early March, Brad and Bob Randall took a series of reconnaissance flights, during which for the first time Brad practiced his aerial photography. Many of the glaciers and peaks the men found on those flights, they were the first to see. On one thrilling flight, the pilot circled Mount Logan. Brad got his first good look at Lucania and the Chitina valley, photographing madly. With the door off, in the dead of winter, these flights were brutally cold; on one, Randall froze his knee. By the end of March, however, the pilot had flown the whole party into Brad's chosen spot on the glacier they named the Lowell. Beside the team's tents, Brad erected a prefab Beaver Board shack—his "survey office."

For the seven men in the heart of the Saint Elias range, there followed two and a half months of unprecedented adventure. Brad had chosen to pursue the expedition in late winter and early spring for ease of glacier travel, but at times the cold was nearly unendurable. During one ten-day stretch, the temperature ranged between minus 40 and minus 5°F, never climbing to zero.

There were a number of close calls. There was the tent fire, which, if it had not been smothered by Andy Taylor before the flames reached a five-gallon gas can, could have blown up base camp. There was a huge crevasse down which three untethered dogs fell, rescued only after Brad rappelled eighty feet into the fissure and tied the trembling canines to a rope with which his teammates hauled them to the surface. There was an encounter with a massive old grizzly bear, which Bob killed with a perfect shot from the team's 30.06 rifle. (The men dined for days on bear heart and liver, but the bearskin rug they stretched beneath their sleeping bags to ward off the glacial cold proved so full of fleas that the whole camp became infested.)

There was also a seemingly endless idyll of discovery. As Bob reminisced in his memoir:

> Every day we saw magnificent rock and snow peaks, unnamed and new to everyone. . . . There was continuing excitement in being where nobody had been before, and almost every day we discovered a new mountain or a new side glacier. In clear weather the snowy summits stood out magnificently against the blue sky, and even on cloudy days the blue-green ice gleamed.

To cap off the expedition in mid-May, rather than fly out from base camp, Brad divided the team into two parties that would traverse the whole Saint Elias range by separate routes, emerging for prearranged pickups at a pair of widely spaced floatplane landing sites. Should one team get into trouble, the other would know where to search by air.

Bob ended up paired with Johnny Haydon and one other teammate in a virtuoso trek down the Lowell Glacier and the Alsek River, during which the trio man-hauled loads on snowshoes, then backpacked under staggering loads, and finally built a raft of skis, driftwood, and air mattresses on which they crossed the flooding Alsek. In the end, the prescribed pickup lake was covered with ice: Bates and his partners had to wait ten days for the surface to thaw out.

Theirs had been an epic journey. Despite a number of near disasters, not one of the seven men suffered a significant injury. What was more, the trip firmly planted the seed of what would turn out to be Bob and Brad's ultimate adventure, for day after day as they trekked the unnamed glaciers, the two men had stared at the pyramid of Mount Lucania, far to the north. As both men knew, the highest unclimbed peak in North America had never been attempted.

Brad had actually first schemed a Lucania assault the previous autumn, only to run into an awkward obstacle. Sometime in the fall of 1934, an acquaintance named Bill Ladd, having heard of Brad's plans, approached him with a request. Ladd had been with Allen Carpé on Mount Fairweather in 1931, and thus was something of a rival. Older than Brad, he was also an established figure in the American Alpine Club. Now he spoke on behalf of another relatively senior mountaineer, Walter Wood, well entrenched in the upper echelons of both the AAC and the Explorers Club.

Wood was planning his own expedition to Lucania for the summer of 1935, Ladd explained. Would Brad graciously back off and yield to the veteran mountaineer?

Brad's competitive juices flowed. He had tried in 1930, after all, to snatch the prize of Fairweather from the clutches of Carpé, another senior eminence. But now Brad bowed to the unspoken hierarchy of the AAC. He would put off his own Lucania dreams and give Wood the first crack. Meanwhile, he would occupy himself with the blank on the Yukon map.

This delicate compromise actually issued in good feeling: on his way toward Lucania in June 1935, Wood ran into Bob Bates in Whitehorse, headed home after the traverse of the Saint Elias range, and promptly invited him on his expedition. Exhausted by the months he had just spent on unknown glaciers, hoping to get back to his teaching career, Bob declined.

That summer, Wood pursued an attempt on Lucania in the old style, horse-packing in from Kluane Lake nearly fifty miles to an advanced base camp on an ice stream the party named Wolf Creek Glacier. There was one innovative touch to the assault, as Wood had provisions (including fresh eggs and hot biscuits!) dropped in to base camp by parachute. The trouble with Wood's approach, however, was that 16,644-foot Mount Steele stood between him and Lucania.

At the end a month and a half of effort, four members of Wood's team, including the leader, stood on top of Steele, having claimed its first ascent. Beyond them loomed Lucania, darting in and out of clouds and mist, massive and tantalizing, but out of the question. In the November 30, 1936, *Life* magazine—the fabled weekly's second issue—Wood published three pages of pictures with a short text. The last photo showed Lucania from the summit of Steele. "Highest unclimbed mountain in North America is Mt. Lucania . . . ," read the caption. "Expeditionist Wood mapped it from the air. Mt. McKinley in Alaska, highest (20,320 ft.) in North America, and Mt. Logan (19,850 ft.), highest in Canada, have both been scaled. But Mt. Lucania remains virtually impregnable."

Music to Brad's and Bob's ears. Brad had studied the aerial

photos he had taken of Lucania on the 1935 reconnaissance flights, as well as others that Russ Dow had shot with Brad's Fairchild camera in March 1936. (Instructing Dow how to operate the bulky apparatus, Brad had said, "It's easy. Just shoot at *f*8 at a 250th.") Armed with these images, Brad had conceived of a novel approach to the remote and lordly mountain. Rather than pack in from the lowlands—either from Kluane Lake to the east, à la Wood, or from McCarthy to the west, as the 1925 Mount Logan party had—he would hire Bob Reeve to land high on the Walsh Glacier, from which a feasible route seemed to lead up the southern headwall and along the east ridge.

On June 18, 1937, Reeve had done just that, only to find the upper Walsh Glacier reduced to a sea of slush. Five days later, in the riskiest takeoff of his career, Reeve had escaped the prison of his marooning, leaving Bob and Brad to their own devices.

On Lucania, the doctrine of "fast and light" would receive its ultimate test.

THREE

SHANGRI-LA

A T 8,750 feet on the Walsh Glacier, Brad and Bob faced a predicament unprecedented in the history of North American exploration. Never before had adventurers penetrated by airplane to such a remote place, only to discover that the airplane was useless to extricate them from it. To be sure, bush pilots in Alaska and Canada had crashed their planes and walked out from the wreckage—but never from a high, crevassed glacier, and never so far across such difficult terrain.

On June 22, 1937, the nearest human beings to Bob and Brad were miners in the town of McCarthy, eighty air miles west of their glacial eyrie, but considerably more by the route any trek on foot would take them. McCarthy had sprung into being in 1900 when the Bonanza strike, which plumbed a fabulously rich vein of copper ore high on a foothill above the Chitina River valley, gave birth to the Kennecott Copper Company. At peak production in 1916, the mine produced 119 million pounds of copper, worth twenty-nine million in 1916 dollars. The population of the boom town spiked at five hundred in 1920.

It had been McCarthy to which Bob Reeve and Russ Dow had ferried the gear and food for the base camp cache in May. From McCarthy, with Reeve's Fairchild 71 still on skis, the pair had then flown the ton of supplies up to the Walsh Glacier. On their flight in on June 18 in the lighter Fairchild 51, Bob and Brad had passed near McCarthy, but some miles south of it, as Reeve took the shortest route from Valdez to the Walsh.

By 1937, the mining town was all but moribund. After the 1938 season, the once-storied Kennecott mine would shut down. Still, a scattering of hard-on-their-luck prospectors and lonely trappers lingered on in and about McCarthy, reluctant to abandon one of the most beautiful natural settings of any village in Alaska. As far as Bob and Brad were concerned, McCarthy spelled civilization.

The best course of action must have seemed obvious. A hundred-odd-mile hike out to McCarthy would be a genuine ordeal, but the two men had ample gear and food in their cache to pull it off. As they had seen on the flight in, the Walsh Glacier below 8,750 feet swept downhill from east to west in a smooth highway of ice, seamed with the occasional field of crevasses, but contorted by nothing like a major icefall. As it approached its moraine-strewn snout, the Walsh grew ugly, a labyrinth of ice cones, hollows, and glacial pools, coated with loose scree and talus. But some thirty miles below base camp, the Walsh joined the massive Logan Glacier. From that point on out, Bob and Brad would be retracing the route by which the 1925 Mount Logan expedition had fought its way to and from Canada's highest mountain. Any trek Henry Hall had accomplished, Brad and Bob knew they could handle.

Yet today, both men insist that they considered hiking out to McCarthy only during the days that Bob Reeve's escape by plane remained uncertain. On foot with Reeve, the glacial novice terrified of crevasses, the mountaineers would have high-tailed it to McCarthy. Once Reeve was safely airborne, Brad and Bob turned their backs on the McCarthy escape route.

That decision, which could well have had fatal conse-quences, bespeaks not only how comfortable Bob and Brad were in the northern wilderness, but just how intense their passion for Lucania was. Oddly, though, neither man will admit today that ambition dictated the choice. A kind of rationalization seems to have set in. The "nauseating desola-tion of dying masses of ice" that Brad had noted on the flight in, the bleak, vertical valley walls, the "potholes full of horrid muddy water" convinced him that a hike down the Walsh Glacier and Chitina River valley would be a nightmare. As Bob blandly recalls, "Flying in, we said to ourselves, Gee, we don't want to go out that way. The alternative seemed very straightforward."

Nor did this blithe perspective on the men's options emerge only in the rosy glow of retrospect. Writing in his diary on June 22, only half an hour after Reeve's hair-raising takeoff, Brad gazed not west but east, toward the high ridges enfolding Mounts Lucania and Steele:

It is a curious feeling to be all alone, except for one other fellow, on a thoroughly rotten glacier with eighty miles of mountains and an 11,000-foot divide between you and civilization. As Bob just said, "We'll know what it's like to be married after this trip!"

"Civilization," in this entry, means not McCarthy, but Burwash Landing on Kluane Lake, a place neither man had ever visited, and a destination, as they would eventually hike, 156 miles away, not eighty.

The first task the pair undertook was an inventory of their belongings. In the letter to Brad's parents that Reeve carried out with him, the twenty-seven-year-old complained, "Bob and I have enough food to keep an army going a dozen years and enough gasoline to keep us warm for months. We have no dish towels and, unfortunately, we have three left boots and one right one. Russ [Dow] has the rest of the boots in Valdez, Gol Ding it!"

The lack of dish towels was hardly a serious matter, but the boot mixup could have been consequential. Today, neither man has any recollection of what Brad's gripe was about. Fortunately, boots would turn out to be the least of the men's problems on Lucania.

Brad's diary records other minor aggravations vis à vis supplies: "We have just found that all but six pounds of the butter is in Valdez—dammit! So much less to lug!"

Within little more than an hour after Reeve's wobbling takeoff, Brad and Bob set out to reconnoiter the route up the Walsh toward Lucania. Roped together, hiking in snowshoes, they slogged across the still mushy surface of the glacier, which rose at the gentle but steady incline of two hundred feet per mile. There were a few stretches where crevasses posed a threat (indeed, the next evening, Bob fell, unroped, up to his waist in a crevasse only three feet from the men's tent door). The going was relatively straightforward, however, and after two hours Brad and Bob stood four miles closer to the mountain that towered over them on the north.

To mark the route—as they had learned to do on Mount Crillon, beginning with Brad's 1932 effort—they thrust "willow wands" into the snow every hundred feet or so. These were actually machined wooden dowels, three-eighths of an inch in diameter and three feet long, with one end painted black. In good weather, a party following the track of its previous passage had no trouble finding its way along a glacier. A few hours of wind could efface that track entirely, however, and in a whiteout the world turned into a featureless blur, through which not even the keenest dead reckoning could safely guide a pair of wanderers. Over the decades in Alaska, more than a few mountaineers' lives have been saved by a dotted line of willow wands.

Brad and Bob had already identified the key weakness in Lucania's defenses. The mountain's gigantic south face, a full 6,000 feet from base to summit, was self-evidently out of the question, a 45-degree precipice loaded with séracs and ice cliffs ready to collapse. Several days later, in fact, from a parallel perch, the two men watched as the whole face was swept by the thundering wreckage of the biggest avalanche either man had ever seen.

The Walsh Glacier, though, headed in the high ridge that connected Lucania to Mount Steele, eight miles to the northeast. It looked as if the going should be relatively easy, a trudge up a broad boulevard of ice, to the foot of the steep headwall that rose 4,000 feet to that catwalk between the two great mountains. The headwall itself was the question mark. Brad thought a shallow protruding rib ought to provide a safe line between the slide-prone slopes on either side.

The men had decided to ferry fifty days' worth of food to the foot of the headwall, pitching their tent at a spot they would call Basin Camp. Then they would try to haul twenty-five days' food up to the Lucania-Steele ridge. If the going proved too tricky or too slow, the other twenty-five days' food at Basin Camp would afford a fallback reserve. If the headwall proved impossible, there would still be the option of returning to Base Camp and heading west out of the mountains toward McCarthy. That course of action would spell defeat, but allow escape.

Bob and Brad dearly hoped that once they left Base Camp, they would never see it again. This meant that, before hauling their loads up the glacier, they would have to sort through the mountainous cache, deciding on the spot which items to abandon. What it grieved Brad most to leave behind was his large-format Fairchild F-8 aerial camera, which exposed five-by-seven-inch negatives, the first of a series of heavy and expensive apparatuses with which Washburn would capture his matchless aerial images of the mountains of Alaska and the Yukon. He was determined to carry and use a lighter camera, his Zeiss Ikon Maximar, for no matter how trying the circumstances, Brad had already developed a burning passion to bring back good pictures from every one of his expeditions. (The excuses of other explorers who captured only poorly exposed, out-of-focus images of their deeds would form a source of lifelong scorn for Washburn.)

It also seemed poignant to abandon all of Russ Dow's and Norman Bright's gear and clothing. As Brad wrote in his diary on June 24, "It has been a really tragic afternoon— throwing away all of Russ' and Norm's carefully packed clothes. They had done so very much to help make the trip a success."

Bob and Brad did not literally throw away these objects. At the time, they still hoped that Bob Reeve might make another flight in to the Walsh, perhaps in winter when the glacier surface had frozen hard, to retrieve the supplies. To that end, they repacked their cache and covered it neatly with a big tarp to protect it from the weather.

As it turned out, Reeve had had such a scare on the Walsh that he had vowed to stay clear of that neck of the Saint Elias Range for the rest of his life. Brad recalls the pilot later saying, "I'd never go back to that goddamned place if you gave me a million bucks." So spooked was he by his close call, Reeve did not even try to fly by Lucania later in the summer to check up on his castaways. As he rationalized (in Brad's recollection), "Christ, I knew they could take care of themselves. Besides, who the hell would've paid the bill?"

Accustomed as we are to today's high-tech, lightweight expedition gear—to down-filled sleeping bags and Gore-Tex parkas, to nylon ropes and tents, to plastic double boots for alpine climbing, to contoured backpacks—it is worth pausing to make our own inventory of the gear Brad and Bob had at their disposal in 1937. Despite Brad's outcry in his letter to his parents, each man had a pair of shoepacs, heavy boots with rubber lowers, leather uppers, and felt insoles. Somewhat sloppy as footgear, shoepacs feel more like galoshes than proper mountain boots; but they effectively forestall frostbite, and they are rigid enough to take crampons, the sets of metal spikes strapped underfoot that climbers use on ice and hard snow. On the moderately difficult ground of Lucania, they were ideal.

On the Walsh Glacier, Bob and Brad wore bearpaw snow-shoes. With wooden frames lashed with crisscrossing grids of shellacked rawhide strips, attached to the boot with leather bindings, these snowshoes were identical to the footwear of many a trapper in the Canadian wilds dating back to the nine-teenth century. Carrying a heavy pack, one inevitably feels clumsy shuffling along in snowshoes (it takes a while to mas-ter the bowlegged waddle that ensures that the back of the right shoe doesn't land on the front of the left, sending one sprawling), but bearpaws are surprisingly effective on even fairly steep slopes. On the Yukon expedition in 1935, Wash-burn's team had used skis, but there the huge icefields were relatively flat. In 1937, Brad decided that skis would not work as well as snowshoes on Lucania. "We figured that on steep slopes," he recalls, "you could only carry half as much weight on skis as you could on snowshoes."

In an age before down-filled jackets and synthetic fabrics, Brad's and Bob's clothing essentially consisted of layers of wool and cotton. Bob had a caribou hide jacket with a rabbit-fur hood that he would swear by years later. The men's mittens consisted of wool inners and shapeless cotton outers. When it was sunny, both men wore the kind of brimmed cotton hats that Edwardians might have sported in African savannahs. For the cold, Brad had a Royal Canadian Mounted Police hat lined, as he recalls, "with muskrat bellies—apparently the softest fur you can get." Both men used the flimsy, cheap aviation goggles favored by the American military.

The men's tent would create a crucial dilemma. Anticipating a party of four, Brad and Bob had brought a single four-man Logan tent. Nine-feet square, pitched around a central pole and guyed tight with pullouts, made of Egyptian cotton, the tent was monstrously heavy—about sixteen pounds dry and clean, well over twenty when soaked or caked with ice. For only a pair of men, this cotton mansion was too much of a good thing—it pitched so tall that one could stand near the center pole, and dry out wet clothes by hanging them from the ceiling. Bob and Brad could see no way to refashion the tent into a snug two-man model. The sleeping bags, made by the Wood Company, were equally unwieldy. Brad's and Bob's bags were rectangular, wool-lined, hard to compress, and heavy. Though they hauled three sleeping bags up to Basin Camp, the two men decided early on that if they pushed over the Lucania-Steele ridge and east toward Kluane Lake, they would abandon two bags and share the third. Already on June 23, the day after Reeve flew out, Brad's diary notes, "Bob and I have just tried sleeping double, head-to-foot, in one bag. It is not going to be bad at all." (Later he would revise that blithe assertion.)

The men had air mattresses, but these too they would eventually jettison, choosing to sleep instead on the hard racks of their Logan packboards. At six pounds apiece, these were not, by modern standards, ridiculously heavy. But as crude wooden frames to which you lashed all your belongings with cordage, packboards were far less comfortable and far harder to climb in than today's form-fitting nylon packs with internal frames. For stoves, the men used a pair of Primus cookers that burned white gas—an efficient design of Swedish origin that had won favor on the epochal Antarctic expeditions of the first two decades of the twentieth century and that would remain the stove of choice well into the 1960s.

The all-important rope was made of hemp. Despite its diameter of five-eighths of an inch (versus the modern standard of eleven millimeters, or a little less than seven-sixteenths of an inch), Bob and Brad's lifeline was only about one-fourth as strong as the nylon and perlon ropes that would supersede hemp. Every climber in the 1930s knew gruesome tales of ropes breaking under the strain of a long fall. The rope Brad and Bob used, on the other hand, was only 100 feet long; today climbers never venture out with lifelines shorter than 150 feet.

For glacial travel today, climbers tie their ropes into harnesses designed to cradle the hips and waist, then attach a pair of short slings connecting the harness to the rope with prusik knots. The idea is that if you fall into a crevasse, you can use the prusiks (which slide upward on the rope but, when cinched down, hold tight for a downward pull) to climb back out unaided. Bob and Brad's setup was simpler. Each man merely tied the end of his rope around his waist with a bow-line. If his partner fell into a crevasse, the other would halt in his tracks, using his own body as anchor to minimize the fall. Then it would be his duty to pull with all his might to aid the friend's floundering as he tried to thrash his way back to the surface. (The system, however, had been designed for parties of four or more: three men pulling from different directions could hope to haul a fourth out of a crevasse. For a two-man party in the event of a serious crevasse fall, it was virtually useless.)

One last piece of gear, which Brad and Bob pondered abandoning in the cache, but ended up taking with them, would prove pivotal in the weeks to come. This was Russ Dow's thirty-year-old police revolver. The gun was heavy, but Bob thought it might come in handy in the lowlands if the pair grew short on food. There were only about a dozen cartridges in the cache; Bob used up several of these finding out that the revolver shot high and left. From the start, it was understood that Bob—a crack shot who, it will be recalled, had killed a grizzly with one cartridge on the 1935 Yukon expedition—would be the team's marksman.

Bob and Brad's food on Lucania likewise bore little resemblance to the freeze-dried casseroles and energy bars of a modern expedition. The staples in 1937 included such heavy items as canned ham and bacon, dates, fresh and dried meat (some of which had to be thrown out after it spoiled), and canned fruit. Breakfast was inevitably a hot cereal, either cornmeal mush or Cream of Wheat or Maltex, floating in reconstituted Klim, the powdered whole milk that several generations of northern adventurers swore by. (Klim, a company whose brand name is "milk" spelled backwards, went out of business in the early 1960s. On June 28, Brad wrote in his diary, "I have succeeded in collecting enough Klim coupons to get a free electric mixer, and have stored them in my shirt pocket!") Lunch was cheese, chocolate, biscuits, jam, dried fruit, and sardines. There were rice, dehydrated baked beans, macaroni, powdered soups, and canned applesauce for dinner along with the meat. The men's favorite post-prandial drink was a cup of Ovaltine, the malty beverage that American moms once unfailingly brought up their children to despise. The only other hot drinks were cocoa and tea sweetened with sugar; the two men deemed coffee unnecessary. (On June 24, Brad's diary sings the praises of an "Ovaltine orgy . . . a magnificent mixture of it, cocoa, Klim, sugar, and hot water!") All the water the men drank and cooked with, of course, came from pots of snow melted on the Primus. Bob and Brad had included in their stocks not even a pint of the "victory brandy" that was *de rigueur* on other expeditions of the day.

Nor did the two men bother with a medical kit. (Modern Alaskan and Himalayan expeditions typically carry everything from antibiotics and prescription painkillers to plastic splints.) Bob and Brad did not even toss in a bottle of aspirin. "We didn't get headaches," Brad recalls. "We did have a lot of adhesive tape."

To haul their heavy loads up the Walsh Glacier, the pair had flown in a collapsible sledge. On June 24, they put the contraption together and loaded two hundred pounds of gear on it, only to have the thing "collapse as flat as a steamer chair." This was a serious setback. The men pulled the pieces into their tent and set to work repairing the sledge. Brad was surprised and delighted to find in the meager tool kit "a Yankee screw-driver with awls and drills to fit it." Without this implement, repair would have been impossible. The men broke apart their extra pair of packboards and used the wood to reinforce the badly designed device. "The sledge bows are oak; so nothing but a drill could possibly have bored through them," wrote Brad in his diary. "Thanks be to the man who put in that Yankee drill. I think it was Norman Bright. It was not on our list, but it saved the day for us."

In the wake of Reeve's departure, the temperature hovered around freezing, preventing the glacier surface from hardening up, and the weather got worse. "It snowed hard all night," Brad wrote on the morning of June 24. "This is the damnedest neck of the woods for snow, rain, and fog that I have ever seen!" Nevertheless, with their plan of action formulated, the men were in good spirits. "I feel fine tonight," Brad had written the evening before. "Bring on the mountain and we'll give her hell!"

At last the sledging began. On June 25, Bob and Brad managed to haul 325 pounds of gear two and a half miles up the Walsh. There, because of "a nasty side slope," they left half the load in a depot and backpacked the rest up to the point they had reached on their reconnaissance two days before. At 2:00 P.M., the men were back at Base Camp, disheartened to have watched a clear morning deteriorate into another blowing snowstorm. They had been able to regain their tent only thanks to the trail of black-tipped willow wands they had placed on June 23. "I have never seen such endless, rotten weather," wrote Brad. By that afternoon, he noted in his diary, the two men had been on the Walsh Glacier a full week, with relatively little to show for it.

The next day, despite five inches of new snow on the ground and flakes continuing to fall, Brad and Bob sledged another three-hundred-plus-pound load "until we nearly died, for it pushed nearly the whole mountain of loose snow ahead of it." All day they struggled with their relays. In the afternoon the sun broke out, but instead of facilitating the men's progress, it turned the glacial basin into a furnace. Despite the fact that their universe was composed of ice and snow, with the sun out it was almost too hot to move. Bob stripped off his clothes and took a "snow bath" to cool off and clean up.

Yet in a herculean effort that stretched from 3:00 in the morning till nearly 9:00 at night, the pair got most of their supplies up to 9,000 feet, where they pitched their tent and established Camp II. As they became familiar with their trail, they deemed the crevasse risk small enough to dispense with roping up; in any event, it was impossible to man-haul the sledge and stay roped a hundred feet apart and ready to arrest a sudden fall. That evening, Brad made a blasé entry in his diary, "While hauling the last load, Bob fell into a crack up to his elbow, but, as usual, the sledge harness held him."

At Camp II for the first time the men got a good look at the headwall, with its slightly protruding rib. The view was daunting. "Zeus, but that will be a climb!" wrote Brad. "But we've *got to make it!*"

Their minor gain in altitude had won the pair a slight reprieve in terms of snow conditions. During the night of June 26, the temperature dropped below 20°F, the coldest yet. Brad noted a "rock-hard crust" beneath the surface accumulation of new snow. All day on the 27th, however, a "rotten southwester" howled across the glacier. Instead of sledging in the morning, Brad and Bob sorted their gear and food once more, striving to eliminate every inessential ounce. As Brad wrote in his diary, "Our motto from now on is: 'Chuck it out and we won't have to lug it!'"

As always when men work hard in the outdoors, food became a matter of supreme interest to the two climbers. On the 27th, Brad recorded, "So far we have eaten virtually no meat at all except a huge four-pound Hormel ham that is delicious beyond words. The dried beef is disgusting. The lemon powder is wonderful. We are gorging on lemonade all the time, and it's grand in the canteen on the trail for lunch."

That day the weather stayed so foul that Brad and Bob were able to move only a load of gear apiece a mile and a half up-glacier. A few serious crevasses and a steady side slope meant that sledging was out of the question, so the men had to backpack their supplies. Between them, they lugged only ninety pounds—far less than the three-hundred-plus they had dragged on their sledge.

At the pace they were going, which by Bob and Brad's high standards was agonizingly slow, they would not reach the head of the basin until July 1. That would mean having spent thirteen days on the Walsh Glacier without having grappled with the first technical obstacle in Lucania's defenses. The weather continued to bedevil the men. The "rock-hard crust" proved illusory. On June 27, Brad noted, "[I]t is still endless slush from the rain if you dig through only a foot of powder and crust." That evening, he wrote, "I have two blisters on my right foot, and Bob has a sore toe; otherwise we are conditioning very fast."

Finally, on June 28, the men got a day of perfect weather. They were moving by 4:00 A.M. With the thermometer at 12°F, a "marvelous crust" had formed, "through which we broke only three or four inches at worst." To take advantage of such conditions, the men backpacked eighty pounds apiece—prodigious loads, given that Bob weighed only 150 pounds himself, Brad a mere 140. (Among the gear, Brad, always a stickler for precise data, had included a scale for weighing loads.) After dumping their loads, the men returned and packed up everything left in camp, then staggered up-glacier under ninety-pound burdens—pretty much the limit for mountaineers no matter what shape they are in.

Then the weird heat, intensified by the basin's facing south, took over. Wrote Brad in his diary, "I have basked on the sledge as long as I dared in this terrific sun, and we have chatted and loafed and sipped lemonade and nibbled crackers all afternoon." ("Loafed" indeed—after hauling eighty- and ninety-pound loads at more than 9,000 feet!) With this day's effort, Brad and Bob launched a strategy many Alaskan climbers have adopted—to rest or sleep during the day and move at night. In June and July, 350 miles south of the Arctic Circle, even at midnight it never gets darker than dusk, and snow conditions are generally superior in the night.

The fickle weather changed in the late afternoon; by 8:00 P.M. it was once more snowing hard. With their solid day's work under their belts, the men refused to be discouraged. "We have just finished another delicious ham supper," wrote Brad, "with raisins, and pea soup, lemonade, Ovaltine, tea, cocoa, jam, and pilot-crackers. This certainly is the life. The barometer is still high and steady; so we may have a good day tomorrow."

On June 30, plowing through six inches of new snow, the two climbers finally reached the base of the headwall. There they found a protected shelf of snow on which to pitch their Basin Camp. In nine days of all-out effort, they had advanced their campaign against Lucania by a paltry eight miles, though in terms of actual travel, as they had relayed loads, they had covered more than three times that distance. Later that day the two men hauled a second load to their hard-won perch. It would be the last stretch of ground on which they could use their sledge. On July 1, the jerry-rigged contraption became one more piece of debris the two men chucked out. (In 1937, climbers in the remote ranges never dreamed of a day when it would be considered poor style to leave one's trash on the mountain. Well into the 1960s, when a party came upon a previous expedition's junk, its reaction partook more of archaeological wonder than of annoyance. On the South Col route on Everest, it would not be until the mid-1980s that the sheer proliferation of garbage and used oxygen bottles inspired the first cleanup expeditions.)

On July 1, a morning fog slowly dispersed, unveiling a perfect day. Brad and Bob sledged the last of their gear up to Basin Camp, at 10,700 feet. The bizarre subarctic heat reached a new intensity: at 2:00 P.M., Brad's thermometer registered 94°F inside the tent.

During these pivotal days, Brad's diary, normally so full of jaunty asseverations, sprinkled so liberally with his favorite punctuation mark, the exclamation point, betrays a latent anxiety. "The bottom of the ridge is very steep, but we'll get onto it somehow," he writes on June 30. "The conditions are always bad here, but we'll make it somehow," he adds on the same day. On July 1: "What we need now is a few really cold nights. . . . The ridge ahead is not sharp. . . . [I]t should go all right with PATIENCE, which has to be the password on this trip."

By now, chucking out things right and left, Brad and Bob had reduced their worldly belongings to 280 pounds—still far too much to carry in a single load. They hoped to transport all this food and gear 4,000 feet up the shallow rib of the headwall to the top of the ridge connecting Steele and Lucania in three carries, averaging forty-five pounds per man per load. (One can backpack on a relatively flat glacier with double that burden, but not climb a steep slope with technical obstacles on it.) Already the two men had given a name to the camp they so dearly wished to place at 14,000 feet. It was Shangri-La, promising the paradise of high summits and an escape to the east.

Bob recalls the process by which the pair eliminated excess gear. "Brad would say, 'How much gas do you think we need?' I would say so much, and he might say, 'I think we need a little more than that.' Usually we agreed entirely."

After dinner on July 1, taking advantage once more of the better conditions at night, the two men reconnoitered the headwall. The first problem was to cross the *bergschrund,* the gaping crevasse that forms at the base of every alpine cliff where the glacier below pulls away from the immovable mountain itself. Fortunately, the men found a bridge across the 'schrund where ice blocks had slumped into the void and plugged it. Bob and Brad had planned only a short probe, but the snow had hardened up so well that it offered a perfect surface for kicking steps. Here, for the first time, they wore their crampons. They would gladly have abandoned their snowshoes at this point, but both men knew from other Alaskan expeditions that high on wind-swept ridges, you could run into freakish accumulations of soft powder snow.

It was an enchanted evening. Eighty miles to the southeast, they saw Mounts Hubbard and Vancouver tinged with alpenglow. The men climbed in ghostly shadow, but far above them on the left, as late as 10:30 P.M., the distant summit ridge of Lucania caught the last rays of the sun. In only two hours, the men ascended a full 2,000 feet, solving half the headwall. The last stretch was the trickiest, a gauntlet weaving through séracs—huge detached ice blocks teetering ominously on the verge of collapse. Here the men used their axes to carve steps in the hard ice. Best of all, the sérac traverse ended in a small shelf—a perfect campsite in the middle of a slope so steep the men had feared there would be no place to pitch their tent.

On July 2, Brad and Bob once more waited out the heat of the day at Basin Camp. The sky was cloudless. At the very center of the parabolic dish facing the sun that the Walsh Glacier and the southern slopes of Steele and Lucania formed, the men sweated through what Brad mordantly called "the hottest afternoon in northern history." At one o'clock, the thermometer, lying in the snow but exposed to the sun, registered an unthinkable 114°F. (Despite his penchant for making meteorological observations, Brad had to cover up the thermometer so the mercury would not burst the bulb.) "This is the hottest day," wrote Brad in a state of semi-incredulity. "Since we returned at noon, neither of us has dared to go out for fear of getting sunstroke. The tent is a furnace a couple of feet off the floor."

All day the men feared the sun would melt the perfect crust of the slope they had climbed in the night, reducing it to slush like the stuff Reeve's plane had sunk into or, worse, turning it into a deadly avalanche runnel. Yet in the afternoon, the sky clouded up. By 11:00 P.M., the temperature had plunged to a welcome 22°F.

Their marathon workdays had thrown the men off their diurnal schedule—though they knew that from Shangri-La onward they must move not at night (for it would be too cold) but in the daytime. On July 3, they left Basin Camp at 9:30 A.M. Soon the dreaded heat was bathing the headwall, but to Bob and Brad's delight, the kicked steps from the day before stayed firm. Climbing this "golden staircase," as Brad called it, he counted steps, reaching 2,300 before the pair arrived at the cache they had left the day before on the shelf of snow at 12,200 feet. On the dangerous sérac traverse, they had fixed a light rope, anchored with snow pickets and an ice axe, to serve as handrail. Dumping their loads, Brad and Bob paused for a drink. As Brad wrote in his diary, "We were so hot that we made a little hole in the snow, covered it with a tarp, and melted a bucketful of water and had lemonade for lunch!"

Rehydrated, the men climbed back down to make a last ferry up to Ridge Camp, as they had nicknamed their providential perch midway on the headwall. In the snow at what had been Basin Camp they left behind a week's supply of food, eight gallons of white gas, a sleeping bag, and a three-by-five-foot rectangle of cloth they had cut out of the tent floor to save weight. By 9:05 P.M. the men were ensconced at Ridge Camp. The view out the tent door was spectacular: 2,000 feet of empty space beneath them (any trash tossed out of the tent promptly disappeared), with a sideways prospect of the gigantic 6,000-foot south face of Lucania, swept daily by avalanches.

The shelf on which the men had pitched their tent was so

small, they had to shovel for two hours into the drift on the uphill side to make room for it. To stabilize the tent, they deliberately froze the corners into the snow. The open rectangle in the center of the floor actually worked to the men's advantage: as Brad wrote in his diary, "We sleep on one side of it; the kitchen is on the other; and in between we get snow for water."

For the first time the two men slept in a single bag. In *The Love of Mountains Is Best,* Bates recalls the semi-comic struggle this entailed:

> That night we both climbed into the same end of one of our rectangular sleeping bags. We managed to squeeze in, but were so crammed we could barely breathe. That system didn't work. Then Brad seized our pliers and removed the heavy zipper at the bottom. One of us climbed in the top and the other in the bottom; and that way we could fit, with shoulders against feet. As we soon learned, however, one person's head always seemed to be downhill. We drew lots to see who would have which end, but eventually alternated. From then on, that was how we slept (or tried to sleep). Occasionally I would hear Brad mutter something, but sound didn't travel well. I would imagine he was commenting on the snow conditions, when finally it would dawn on me that he was saying, "Quit kicking me in the ear!"

(On June 23, it will be recalled, Brad's diary had recorded a first experiment in sleeping head-to-toe, two in a single bag. No doubt it was then that Brad made the crucial zipper alteration, not at Ridge Camp.)

The men were exhausted from their 2,000-foot carries up from Basin Camp in the glacial heat. "Now for supper," wrote Brad that evening. "We're both sunburned like lobsters and hungry as bears. This morning I put too much salt in the cereal, and so we had only one nasty cup apiece."

The airy perch on which the men had pitched their tent, after fifteen consecutive nights spent in mundane camps on the gentle Walsh Glacier, lent a certain edge to their mood. So did the uncertainty of their fate, which here reached a critical pivot point. Brad's diary betrays that edginess: "Goodness only knows, we've worked to get here; I wonder when the weather will let us reach that pass [between Steele and Lucania]. It will be the thrill of my whole life to realize that there is nothing but downhill to Burwash! . . . We are half way up now, and we're ready to *siege* the last half if we have to. Powder snow is likely to be our worst enemy from here on up."

It was a canny prognosis. That night, to the men's dismay, clouds rolled in and it began snowing hard, without a breath of wind. "This would be a wild spot in a real blow," Brad had written just as the snow began to fall on July 3. By noon on the 4th, an outlandish twenty inches of new snow had been dumped on the men's precarious camp. The tent itself was nearly buried. Both men knew that such a snowfall could turn any slope into an avalanche trap. Only the shallow bulge of the rib they had chosen for their route up the headwall offered protection from a universe of sliding snow.

Most climbers would have waited out such a storm, and even given the slopes a day or two of good weather to slough clear and firm up. Committed to their minimalist assault, however, Brad and Bob felt they could not waste a single day.

At half past noon, they started up the rib above Ridge Camp. At once they floundered in knee-deep snow; in protected hollows, they plunged in waist deep. The men stayed roped, a hundred feet apart, a necessary precaution, for, as Brad wrote later that day, "We fell in half a dozen snow-covered cracks, but only to our waists."

To the men's joy, however, the slope seemed safe from avalanches. For more than two hours, they staggered clumsily upward, plowing a trench through the powder, taking turns in the lead. Slowly the snowfall ebbed and the clouds began to break. Having started in virtual whiteout, the pair were startled to catch sudden glimpses of their camp far below, "perched [as Brad wrote] on the edge of nothing," and of the upper reaches of Lucania, "soaring skyward, wreathed in blowing snow and mist."

Thirteen hundred feet above Ridge Camp, at an altitude of 13,500 feet, the angle of the rib abruptly relented. The triage by which the two men had discarded much of their gear but kept what they deemed essential now proved sagacious, for on this gentler slope, loaded even deeper with powder snow, Brad and Bob could advance only by donning the bearpaw snowshoes they had lugged all the way to this point (and had had the wit to pack with them that morning).

They could almost taste Shangri-La. The slope here was too gentle to slide, and only scattered, harmless séracs littered the landscape. Rounding one of the last of these ice blocks, they saw an easy route to within fifteen feet of clear sailing—except that, in Brad's words, "those fifteen feet were a crack at least sixty feet deep, with an absolutely impassable vertical wall!" In the end, the men had to retreat, then make a mile-long detour to circumvent this crevasse.

Instead of reaching Shangri-La in a single push from Ridge Camp, the pair realized they would need an intermediate camp at 13,800 feet. "All we did today," wrote Brad dispiritedly back in the tent late that afternoon, "was to make certain of our route above here, and to break out a preliminary trail, which I fear will be all gone tomorrow, for it is still snowing. I've never seen a place where it snowed so continually." Even dinner, to which the men had looked forward all day, was disappointing: "Dammit, about one-third of our two-pound tin of butter is rancid from roasting in the sun in a duffel bag yesterday; but we have cut off the outside and the center is all right. We are cooking Knorr's soup and the dried beef together (after boiling the soup and soaking, wring[ing] the salt from, and frying the beef); the beef is pretty tasteless alone."

As they lay in their tent, the men heard the thunder of nearly nonstop avalanches all around them, most of them sweeping the east face of Lucania. "They sound like great freight trains which slowly get louder," wrote Brad, "and then fade away once more into silence, leaving only the continual patters of the snowflakes on our roof."

Characteristically, instead of crawling into their single bag after dinner and trying to sleep, the men went back out into the storm. Desperate lest the new snow fill in the track they had so laboriously plowed that afternoon, they pushed themselves close to the limit to get another load up to the gear dump at 13,800 feet. It took them two hours and forty-five minutes to climb those 1,500 feet, but only twenty-five minutes to descend.

At last something like normal subarctic temperatures seemed to have descended on the Saint Elias Range. That night the thermometer dropped to 2°F, by far the coldest yet. When a morning sun burned through the clouds on July 5, for the first time Brad and Bob greeted its warmth gratefully. The cold also served to consolidate the still-perilous slopes. That day, the men wrestled their last loads up to what they were calling Ice-Block Camp at 13,800 feet "in one dreadful two-hour-and-fifteen-minute haul." They pitched their tent in the lee of one of the biggest séracs (whence the name for the camp). That evening, optimism reigned, yet it was still laced with uncertainty. "Only a mile to Shangri-La—" wrote Brad in his diary, "in fact, only a hundred yards—but we have to go a mile to get there! I wonder when that great day will come."

Thanks to the men's persistence, the great day came on the morrow. Neither man slept well during the night, as snow fell once more. In the morning the sky was "very grey and forbidding" (in Brad's words), and lenticular cloud caps—nearly certain harbingers of a coming storm—covered the summits of Steele and Lucania. Nonetheless, Bob and Brad packed up fifty pounds apiece and started off through the deep snow, circling via their long detour around the impassable crevasse. "At one point Bob fell into his shoulders into a tremendous crack," reported Brad. (On this expedition, Bates seems to have suffered by far the majority of the crevasse falls. Was this just his bad luck, or did the fact that he weighed ten pounds more than Washburn mean that he broke through snow bridges that Brad could walk across unscathed?)

Yet the going got easier and easier, as the slope gentled almost to level. By late morning on July 6 the two climbers stood on the crest of the long ridge between Steele and Lucania. *"We have made Shangri-La!"* Brad later crowed in his diary. It was the nineteenth day after Bob Reeve's landing in the slush of the Walsh Glacier.

Bob remembers that triumphant moment: "We didn't shout for joy. We just said, 'Well, this is it. We made it. From here on, we know what we want to do.'"

F O U R

OVER THE TOP

I T took another day, and three more load carries, for Brad and Bob to establish themselves at Shangri-La. The next-to-last haul, in the late morning of July 7, took place in the middle of a "wild snowstorm." Wrote Brad in his diary, "We could not see a thing either way—just kept to the down-hill side of the willow wands and scuffed along in the snow, feeling for yesterday's steps. . . . [W]e couldn't even tell we were on a grade when we crossed the 45 [-degree] traverse under the séracs. It feels like walking in a cloud and it is very hard to maintain balance."

Then, as they rested in the tent at Ice-Block Camp before packing up the last load, a huge sérac collapsed nearby— "we could feel the ice jerk underneath us," noted Brad. (Over the years, many climbers have been crushed to death by falling séracs. Usually their bodies are unrecoverable.)

The significance of reaching Shangri-La was monumental. Brad and Bob had placed their camp only three miles southwest of the summit of Mount Steele. Before the expedition, Brad had made a small album of the twelve best aerial photos of the Lucania region that he and Russ Dow had shot in 1935 and 1936, respectively. One of the pictures in that album now made it clear that there would be no difficulty in traversing beneath the summit of Steele on the north. Once they had gained Steele's northeast ridge, they would intersect the route by which Walter Wood's party had made the mountain's first ascent in 1935. And, as Brad and Bob were fond of repeating to each other, with the cockiness of their youthful expertise, "Anything Walter Wood can climb up, we can climb down."

The dangerous campaign of the last seven days, however, as the men had fought through storms to carry loads up the 4,000-foot headwall, ought to have given the conclusive lie to Brad and Bob's rationalization that climbing to the Steele-Lucania col to launch a long eastward trek toward Burwash Landing was the safest and easiest way out of the Saint Elias Range. Yet Brad's diary never addresses the question, and today both men still insist that it looked as though it would have been harder and nastier to flee west down the Walsh Glacier toward McCarthy.

The real motivation for reaching Shangri-La, of course, was to have a crack at North America's highest unclimbed mountain. Despite all the handicaps with which the fickle weather had shackled the men, they were not yet willing to abandon the expedition's original goal just to ensure an outcome so mundane as survival.

Late on July 7, as the storm that the lenticular clouds had presaged smothered the exposed Lucania-Steele ridge, Brad and Bob hunkered down in the tent at Shangri-La, while Brad made a long entry in his diary. With his passion for precise detail, he took stock not only of the men's food and gear, but of their prospects.

They were short, Brad noted, on sugar, butter, and cereal, but had plenty of beans, soup, bacon, and the detested dried beef. As they had planned, they had managed to haul twenty-five days' worth of food to the high camp. Yet now they faced a cruel imperative. For all the chucking out of supplies the men had practiced over the previous two weeks, they still had well more than a hundred pounds apiece of gear and food. Once they began their descent of Mount Steele, they were determined to reduce their burdens to a single load apiece, preferably of no more than sixty pounds. It would be far too arduous, as well as too perilous, to double- or triple-pack loads *down* that unseen ridge. From the shoulder of Steele to Kluane Lake, the men's guiding doctrine of "fast and light" would rule every hour.

It may be, moreover, that the two men miscalculated how many days their food was actually good for. A kindred error has dogged the heels of some of the most seasoned explorers: it led directly to the deaths of Robert Falcon Scott and his four companions on their return from the South Pole in 1912. Under normal circumstances, it is hard for an average-sized man to burn more than 4,500 calories a day, even with all-out exertion. Most expedition rations are planned to supply about that many daily calories in food. Yet for men in superb condition, working in the cold as hard as Bob and

Brad were, it is possible to burn as many as 6,000 calories a day. A man eats and eats and never sates his hunger. What was more, Bob and Brad were lean, almost skinny, at the outset of the Lucania trip: they had precious little body fat to burn.

Brad's long July 7 diary entry breathes a deep sigh of relief. "It's a glorious feeling actually to be camped here, with no more of the grueling uphill that we have had up till now. The tension is relaxed." In his ebullience, Brad understates the task ahead: "Only a 2,000-foot spur [the shoulder of Steele] separates us from downhill to Burwash, and there isn't a crack between us and it. We certainly have fought to get here and I think that what we have done is downright amazing, considering that we have had fresh snow every single day so far, with the exception of one."

In the very next breath after declaring the tension relaxed, Brad comes to his senses: "Four men would have made a world of difference. With only two, no one can relax and take a breather; it is just a continual fight. But so far we've won."

While Brad was writing in his diary, Bob took the trouble to shave (exactly how he did so, with snowmelt for water and no soap or shaving cream, has escaped both men's memories). Wrote Brad of his partner's effort to maintain a civilized toilette, "I shaved at the Ice-Block Camp and Camp III; so I'm still one up on him, but we certainly are some specimens, on account of peeling sunburn and windburn."

Other climbers, facing a plight similar to Brad and Bob's, have felt their nerves fray to the breaking point. Cabin fever all too easily sets in, so that a teammate's mildest habits drive one to the edge of apoplexy. Two men sleeping head-to-toe in a single inadequate bag make a perfect recipe for such inter-personal antagonism.

Perhaps the single most remarkable aspect of the Lucania expedition is that both men swear they never felt a moment's antipathy toward each other, let alone indulged in an overt quarrel. "I can't recall an evil word from the beginning to the end of that trip," insists Brad today. "We got along very well," says Bob blandly. "I don't think we had any disagreements."

If this is true—and not some rose-tinted distortion in the glow of memory, or the residue of an ethic of the day that one never airs in public the dirty linen of a private adventure—then the remarkable harmony the two men enjoyed during the most hazardous exploit of their lives owes much to a happy symbiosis between their temperaments.

Early and late, Brad Washburn was notorious for the obstinacy of his will. On an expedition, one pretty much did things his way or not at all. Brad could lead brilliantly, but not follow, and it is not surprising that he was the leader or co-leader of every expedition he ever went on. On Mount Crillon in 1933, Washburn locked horns with a similarly obstinate teammate two years his junior, Charlie Houston. Houston would go on to make the first ascent of Mount Foraker, Alaska's third-highest peak, and to co-lead the 1938 and 1953 American K2 expeditions with Bates. But though the two men have remained loyal friends all their lives, Houston and Washburn never climbed together again after 1933.

Bob Bates was the temperamental opposite of Washburn. A peace-at-all-costs go-between, he more than once interceded gently and wisely between expedition teammates who were on the verge of serious conflict. The phrase "the nicest guy you'll ever meet" comes readily to the lips of most of Bates's lifelong friends.

If this suggests a certain acquiescent passivity about the man, that was not the case in the mountains. The last person in the world to speak ill of another (*The Love of Mountains Is Best* is serenely free of rancor throughout its 493 pages), the first to volunteer for any dirty or dangerous job, Bates possessed a will in its own way as strong as Washburn's. And Bob had a valuable quality that Brad entirely lacked. In an ominous or uncertain fix, Bob summoned up a Zen-like equanimity. If a predicament was beyond his control, he accepted the fact. Stoicism of this sort makes a powerful antidote to paralyzing fear.

As Bob puts it today, "I take things in stride. If I can't do anything about [the situation], I don't worry."

Brad, on the other hand, found it hard to relax when matters were beyond his control. Just as he insisted on being the leader, he felt a nagging anxiety when he could not bend the world to fit his will. And he was the soul of impatience. In a 1983 interview in *American Photographer*, alluding to his camera work, he acknowledged as much: "A lot of people have said to me, 'You must have an enormous amount of patience.' Actually, I'm impatient as hell. I'm just stubborn."

There was another ingredient to the two men's remarkable rapport on Lucania. During their downtime on the mountain, when they lay in their tent waiting out storms—those moments when it is easiest to get on each other's nerves—they whiled away the hours singing cowboy songs and railroad ballads out loud together, for which music they shared an inexhaustible zest. "The Wreck of the Old '97," "Ain't Got No Use for the Women," "Casey Jones," "The Red River Valley," "The Wreck of the CNO No. 5." (Reminiscing in Bates's living room in New Hampshire in the winter of 2000, Bob and Brad suddenly burst into dual concert: "I awoke one morning on the Old Chisholm Trail / With a rope in my hand and cow by the tail / Come a ki yi yippee yippee yay, yippee yay / Come a ki yi yippee yippee yay / There's a stray in the herd, and the boss said kill it / So I slammed it in the ass with the handle of a skillet / Come a ki yi yippee yippee yay . . .")

As Brad's July 7 entry makes clear, the pull of the escape route that lay just beyond their tent door at Shangri-La was powerful. In two days, the men sensed, they could be off Steele and back in the lowlands, with nothing but a long hike between them and Kluane Lake. At 14,000 feet on a windswept ridge, moreover, with a tent missing half its floor, a single sleeping bag that could not be zipped closed, and no air mattresses, Bob and Brad were in an exceedingly vulnerable position. All day on the 7th it snowed, and that night the temperature plunged to minus 1°F.

Yet the men were determined to have a stab at Lucania. On July 7, the 17,150-foot summit lay more than 3,000 feet above them and five miles away, invisible in the storm. Any attempt, the two men agreed, would require an intermediate camp. This in turn raised the specter of an insidious scenario. The broad ridge on which they had pitched their tent at Shangri-La was almost featureless, one stretch of billowing snow looking just like the next. To make another camp closer to Lucania, they would have to carry their tent with them, leaving the rest of their belongings in a cache at Shangri-La. On other expeditions, Bob and Brad had seen just how quickly blowing snow on a high ridge could drift over any object that protruded from the surface. If the storm continued as it had the last several days, with Brad and Bob camped several miles closer to Lucania, they could well lose their Shangri-La cache for good. They had only their three-foot willow wands to mark the depot of supplies.

Undaunted, the two men set out after dinner on July 7, with light snow falling, to carry a load of gear and food toward Lucania. The going was as bad as they might have feared: eighteen inches of new snow, with soft stuff beneath, once more requiring snowshoes. In three hours, they were back at Shangri-La, having deposited ropes, crampons, and eight days' worth of food on a swale two miles closer to the summit. (It was not so much that Brad and Bob thought it would really require eight days from Shangri-La to get up Lucania, as that the food was in any case expendable, since they could not carry all twenty-five days' worth down Mount Steele.)

Yet the next day Brad indicated in his diary just how strong the habit of frugality had become for these men living on the edge: "We are trying to save food. We each put one quarter of a teaspoonful of sugar in our cereal (which we have sweetened a bit with raisins); and we save the cereal pot to cook the soup in for lunch and supper, and wash it only once a day." Because of the weather, the men remained pessimistic. The night before, Brad had closed his long diary entry with "That wind simply must change or we haven't a prayer. Ovaltine and bed."

Through most of July 8, the men "loafed" (Brad's usual word for anything other than all-out activity) as they peeked periodically out the tent door to check on the weather. At last their wait was rewarded, when, just before 4:00 P.M., the snow stopped falling and the clouds peeled rapidly away. Despite the intense cold, Brad and Bob packed up their tent after a quick dinner and set off toward their cache of gear two miles to the southwest. When they arrived there, instead of camping on the spot, they loaded up the food, ropes, and crampons and pushed on. By 10:00 P.M., they were three and a quarter miles from Shangri-La, camped at the very base of Lucania's summit pyramid. Inside the tent, it was zero degrees Fahrenheit, and an icy wind out of the northeast drilled the cotton walls of their shelter, but the sky remained gloriously clear.

That night the thermometer crept down to minus 8°F. It was impossible for the men to stay warm with their skimpy gear: as the hours passed, the vigil felt more like a bivouac than a normal night in a tent. By 9:00 in the morning on July 9, the temperature was up to a plus 6°F, and the day was still perfectly clear.

From the moment the two left the tent, they were forced to plow along with their snowshoes on. "I doubt if Lucania is ever anything but powder," Brad later wrote. "It was waist-deep flour with not a trace of crust anywhere." For four hours, the men inched laboriously ahead, changing the lead often. "One of us would get so pooped that he couldn't move," Brad remembers, "and he'd step aside, and then the other guy would do it for a while." In his diary, Brad recorded, "We fought on as I have never fought in my life."

The northeast ridge of Lucania unfolds in a long string of subsidiary summits. Rather than climb over each and have to descend into the gap beyond, Bob and Brad skirted several of these subsummits by traversing across a plateau on the north. After four hours, the men bent their course south and upward to aim at a saddle between two of the highest false summits of Lucania. As they neared that saddle, the slope grew steeper and steeper, until they were forced to traverse "a 40 [-degree] sideslope of fathomless powder, veneered with an inch of rock-hard wind-crust."

Such terrain was impossible to negotiate in snowshoes. In the lead, Brad took his bearpaws off, hoping the crust would support his weight. All at once he plunged through to his knees, so suddenly that he dropped his snowshoes. With a sinking heart, he watched them slide toward the void below— only to fetch up a mere ten feet away on an imperceptible bulge. Gingerly, he crept down and retrieved the invaluable footgear.

There was only one way to proceed. With his snowshoes back on, Brad used his ice axe to smash away the inch-thick crust ahead of him. Gaining only a few feet with each flurry of axe blows, he waddled forward in the powder two feet below the surface. In effect, he was carving a trench through the fiendish snowscape. It took Brad an hour to advance a mere hundred yards. It was the hardest single passage the men had confronted during their twenty-two days on Lucania, and it had to be performed in the rarefied air of 16,000 feet.

Exhausted, Brad turned the lead over to Bob. Finally, at 2:25 in the afternoon, the pair topped out on the saddle. They let out what Brad later called "a loud huzzah" and collapsed to rest. After five-and-a-half nonstop hours of struggle, they indulged in a snack of chocolate, dates, and raisins. There was not a breath of wind, and the day was holding perfect.

At last, on this final ridge, a true crust gave the men the break they needed. They put on their crampons and started on. The steel points bit cleanly into the hard snow, and the crust failed to collapse beneath their weight. Ahead, the last subsummit beckoned. Near its crest, the ridge serpentined into a plume that seemed to overhang, giving Brad and Bob a last grave doubt about their success. But that apparent overhang was a trick of foreshortening. When they confronted a plume that was merely steep, they found they could crampon right up it.

The true summit looked about a mile away. The intervening ridge was seamed with a few small bands of rock—"the first rock we have seen anywhere for nearly four weeks," Brad later wrote. Skirting these bands on the left, the men marched forward with a growing elation. Brad's diary entry late that evening captures the mood of the moment: "It seemed like a dream—the two of us approaching the top of Lucania, with no more difficulties in sight. . . . We did not want to lose our mountain this time. We both knew that if we failed on this try, we'd probably be too tired to take another crack at it before the weather changed; we were still, as we had been all day, desperately serious."

At 4:30 P.M.—they had been going for seven and a half hours with only one short break—the men, still roped together, topped a feathery cornice and stood on what they assumed was the summit, only to see yet another, slightly higher crest ahead of them. They stifled their cry of joy and trudged on.

It was a short-lived disappointment. Ten minutes later, Bob and Brad laid the first human footprints on the summit of

Mount Lucania. "[O]ur yell of triumph could have been heard in Timbuctoo!" Brad later bragged to his diary.

The hour the men spent on top would turn out to be one of the most magical of their lives. In the cloudless air, a stunning panorama of glaciated peaks ranged about them on all sides. Far to the southeast, 190 miles away, they could see Mount Fairweather, the first Alaskan mountain Brad had attempted, in 1930. Much closer, to the south, sprawled the summit plateau of Mount Logan, the biggest mountain in the world, in terms of sheer bulk, over the right shoulder of which they stared at the graceful summit pyramid of Mount Saint Elias, whose first ascent by the Duke of the Abruzzi in 1897 had launched mountaineering in the Far North of North America. Off Logan's left shoulder, they saw the peaks in the Yukon that Brad and Bob and their teammates in 1935 had been the first men to approach: Alverstone, Hubbard, Seattle, and many more, some still unnamed.

The men could also see, twisting darkly far below them away to the west, the Chitina valley that had given them such gloomy pause on the flight in with Reeve on June 18. And in the opposite direction, to the east, they caught a glimpse of the lowlands they would have to traverse to reach Kluane Lake. Only there had the weather turned bad, as they peered down on what Walter Wood had named Wolf Creek Valley, "black with pouring rain," in Brad's phrase. "Oh, what a relief to know that it could be warm enough to rain somewhere!"

Before they left the summit, Brad was determined to take a team portrait. It was not an easy task, for in the zero-degree air his Zeiss camera had frozen. He found that he could make the shutter work only at 1/200th of a second.

No problem. Brad tied the camera to the top of his axe with a shoelace, got himself and Bob into position, and activated the self-timer. The summit photo from Lucania on July 9, 1937, was the best taken to that date on any mountaintop in Alaska or the Yukon. It remains to this day a masterly evocation of radiant exuberance (see photo insert). In it, perfectly exposed in razor-sharp black-and-white, Brad and Bob stand shoulder-to-shoulder, almost at attention. An ice axe is planted between the men, exactly on the summit. Brad carries coils of the hemp rope over his right shoulder. He holds his hat in his right hand, while Bob's hood is pulled off his head. Brad's hair is tousled with the wind, but Bob's looks almost combed in a neat rightward swoop. Both men grin wearily but with utter joy at the camera, as the strain of twenty-two days of struggle and uncertainty shows in the creases in their weather-beaten faces. As much as an image of triumph, the photo forms an icon of ideal friendship.

Ironically, on the same day that Brad and Bob reached the summit of Lucania, Bob Reeve wrote a letter to Brad's mother (who had written him, expressing concern about her son). Perhaps the pilot was nagged by guilt for not having checked up on the charges he had left on the Walsh Glacier three weeks earlier, for in the letter he reassures Brad's mother far more blithely than he had any business doing:

Don't worry about the boys, Mrs. Washburn, for they are experienced and competent and now that they are above where it is ice and hard snow, their going should be plenty fast. It was only about a three days' job for them to establish

1

Valdez, Alaska, as it looked in 1937. The mud flats from which Bob Reeve took off are in the left background, beyond the town.

Bush pilot Bob Reeve in front of his Fairchild 51 airplane.

2

Bob Bates (left) and Brad Washburn.

Washburn with his fifty-three-pound Fairchild camera, with which he took the aerial photos that unlocked the secrets of Mount Lucania.

3

4

Reeve in front of his plane, sunk in the slush on the Walsh Glacier, 5
June 18, 1937.

6

Mount Lucania from the southeast, with Washburn and Bates's route
and principal camps indicated.

Mt. Lucania

to Mt. Steele >

Shangri-La
Camp

Basin Camp

< △ to Base Camp

7

Washburn and Bates in their single sleeping bag before they figured out how to sleep in it head to foot.

Looking toward Mount Lucania from the northeast, at the Shangri-La camp at 14,000 feet, July 7, 1937.

8

Bob Bates and Brad Washburn atop Mount Lucania on July 9.

9

Mounts Lucania (left) and Steele, seen from the east. The route of Washburn and Bates's descent from Steele is the curving ridge in the right center.

10

(right) *Burwash Landing on Kluane Lake, in the Yukon Territory.*

The snout of the Donjek Glacier, site of the miserable bivouac on July 14. The next day, the two men forded the Donjek River just beyond the snout, in the left middle ground.

Gene Jacquot and his family, Burwash Landing.

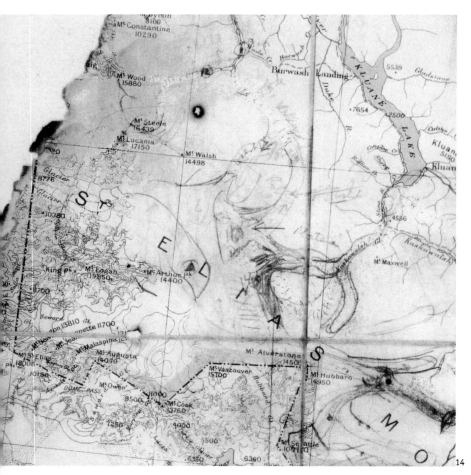

14

The only map that Bates and Washburn had for their journey. On the 1935 Yukon expedition, the map had partially burned in a camp fire. Washburn's pencil sketches of previously unknown glaciers fill in some of the blanks.

Brad Washburn, Alaska, July 2001, planning the flight to retrace the route of the 1937 expedition. (Photo by David Roberts)

15

a camp at that level and they will work early mornings and nights when there is a good crust. I, personally, think that it is a certainty they will make Lucania for the approach from where we landed them was almost perfect and fast travelling.

Reeve was either talking through his hat (for at the time he fled the Walsh on June 22, he had no knowledge of conditions higher on the mountain, and good reason to fear the worst) or telling an anxious mother what he thought she wanted to hear. "Nine-tenths of their battle was over when they landed on Walsh Glacier," Reeve added. This was patent nonsense— as no doubt Brad's mother suspected.

The pilot closed with a jaunty encomium: "You may well be proud of your boy, Mrs. Washburn, for, as I wired the Associated Press, Father Hubbard and Admiral Byrd are pikers compared with Brad Washburn and Bob Bates." (Father Bernard Hubbard was a pioneering explorer of the Aleutian chain, who had written a popular book about the region, called *Cradle of the Storms*.)

On the descent, Brad and Bob stopped at the rock bands on the summit ridge, where they prized loose a pair of chunks of black schist, as mementos of consolation to give to Norman Bright and Russ Dow. Most of the way down, they were forced to wear their snowshoes, which made for delicate going on the side slopes. Something was wrong with the binding on Bob's left snowshoe, for the bearpaw kept falling off. It was not until 8:20 P.M., after eleven and a half hours of arduous struggle, that the two men regained camp. "We barely had our boots off before falling asleep," remembers Bob; but Brad's diary records a celebration of sorts: "And then came quantities of beans, tea, and cocoa brewed from the chocolate in an empty butter tin—and singing old Western Range songs— and a glorious sunset—and, finally, to bed at 10:30."

In the night the thermometer dropped to minus 10°F, the coldest the men had yet experienced on Lucania, and a sharp wind rose out of the north. Next morning, Brad and Bob performed a further triage on their supplies. They discarded all the white gas they had carried to this supplemental camp, as well as all the food save some soup, bacon, sugar, and beef. Bone-tired from the previous day's effort, they nonetheless got off by 10:15 A.M. and, lugging fifty-pound loads, arrived at Shangri-La in only two hours.

If ever a pair of climbers had earned a rest day, Brad and Bob were now entitled to one. But they were still in a vulnerable position, and as long as the weather held good, they felt they could not afford to "loaf." In the late afternoon of July 10, the men carried forty pounds apiece over to the base of Mount Steele, marking the trail with willow wands until, just short of where they dumped their loads, they used up the last of the hundreds of black-tipped dowels they had brought along to demarcate their route. There was a certain poetic justice in this economy, for that ferry toward Steele would be the last time Brad and Bob would have to retrace their steps.

From the base of Steele, for the first time, the men caught a glimpse of Kluane Lake, the goal of their escape, nestled among low green hills to the east—only fifty-five miles away in a direct air line, but much farther by any overland route the men could devise. Having taken in that tantalizing view, the pair dashed back to Shangri-La. That night the temperature dropped to minus 9°F, and the tent flapping in the bitter north wind made it hard to sleep—as did the men's hopes of getting all the way down Steele's northeast ridge on the morrow.

They were up at 6:30 in the morning, but waited almost three hours for their world to warm up before setting out. In the meantime Brad recorded the scene: "My, but it was cold writing this diary last evening when we returned. We have a deep pit in the middle of the tent, in which we put the stove. Then we sit on packboards, dangling our legs by the stove, while we alternately drink hot Ovaltine and cocoa, warm our hands and diaries, and write them bit by bit." (One would give much to be able to read Bates's diary from Lucania, but somewhere over the ensuing years, perhaps in a change of residence, the little book was lost.)

At 9:15 in the morning, the men set off. The temperature had warmed to 8°F, but the incessant north wind, driving gales of spindrift across the ridge, made for chilly going. Following their own broken trail, the men took only an hour and ten minutes to reach their gear dump from the evening before. They lashed these supplies to their already laden packboards, hoisting burdens of seventy-five pounds each—more than they liked for what promised to be a tricky descent of Steele's northeast ridge.

The men's initial plan had been simply to contour around Steele's summit pyramid on the north, but now, with the weather holding clear, the chance to bag the second ascent of the 16,644-foot peak proved irresistible. Bob and Brad detoured laboriously upward to the crest of the Steele ridge, dumped their packs, and in twenty minutes virtually waltzed to the top. The last stretch required crampons and a bit of step cutting with the ice axe, but presented no real technical difficulty.

On top, the men were stunned to discover, sticking out of the snow, the upper few inches of a bundle of willow wands left by Walter Wood's party two years before. The find belied the wisdom of the day (to which Bob and Brad subscribed), that the vagaries of storm and snowfall caused the summits of great glaciated mountains to rise or shrink substantially from year to year. Instead, it seemed that some mysterious parsimony of wind conspired with the mountain's shape to keep the summit drifts nearly as stable as the tops of mountains made entirely of rock. Beyond that geological surprise, however, lay one of purely emotional impact: the willow wands were the first sign of human presence not their own that Brad and Bob had seen in twenty-four days.

Once more Brad contrived a summit photo, this time with the men kneeling behind the bouquet of the upright willow wands. The smiles on their faces look far more relaxed than the weary grins of two days before.

Back at their packs, the men sorted out their belongings one last time, determined to chuck out enough food and gear to reduce their loads to sixty pounds each. They discarded one rucksack (the cloth pack each man used for lighter loads than those that required a packboard) and four pounds of food; they cut out the rest of the tent floor, threw away the tent pegs, and even cut the guy strings off the tent. They were left with a mere half gallon of white gas and nineteen pounds of food, as well as a tent that it would now be next to impossible to pitch properly. They did not abandon, however, Brad's precious Zeiss camera, with his last three film packs, nor Russ Dow's heavy police revolver and the eight or ten cartridges that remained. At last the loads were down to sixty pounds each.

On the face of it, nineteen pounds of food would seem to be stretching the pair's margin awfully thin. Working as hard as they were, Brad and Bob were consuming at an absolute minimum two or two and a half pounds of food each per day. That would mean that nineteen pounds of rations would last only four or five days.

The men had, however, an ace up their sleeve. They knew that Walter Wood's party, supported not only by pack train but by supplies parachuted in, had had an excess of food by the time it was done with Steele. They knew Wood had left a substantial cache of food behind, emergency rations for some future party. And they knew precisely where that cache was, on a grassy bench above the right edge of the Wolf Creek Glacier where it bent to the east only fifteen miles from the base of Steele's northeast ridge.

Brad and Bob began the descent at 3:30 P.M. on July 11. They covered the first 2,000 vertical feet in snowshoes, despite the steepness of the terrain. At 14,500 feet, a gentle plateau suddenly gave way to a sharp ridge. Here, at last, the men dared abandon the bearpaws without which they would never have been able to reach Shangri-La, let alone climb Lucania and Steele. They switched to crampons and started down the curving crest of the ridge.

The men's blithe conviction that "anything Walter Wood can climb up, we can climb down" notwithstanding, it is a far more difficult proposition to descend a route one has never seen before than to ascend it in the first place. From below, a ridge gives away its secrets: a pair of binoculars can usually make plain the traverses that lead to dead ends, the towers that can be circumvented. From above, on the other hand, a ridge unfolds beneath you as a series of nearby cusps and brows, each eclipsing the hidden snags below.

All the way down Steele's northeast ridge, Bob took the lead, held on a tight belay by Brad. With more Alaskan experience and his teenage training in the Alps, Brad felt perhaps more comfortable in the role of the partner entrusted with stopping any fall; but Bob had an uncanny instinct for route-finding. Now, at regular intervals, the men pulled out Brad's album of aerial photographs, trying to correlate their position on the ridge with these omniscient mountainscapes. Each time Bob approached a blank edge, the men felt a heightened tension. Then Bob would call out "Okay!" or "All's well ahead!" and the tension would ebb.

On July 7, Brad had predicted that from the shoulder of Steele to Burwash Landing, "there [won't be] a crack between us and it." He was quite wrong. At 12,000 feet, Bob entered a zone where vexsome crevasses covered with thin snow bridges lay directly athwart the knife-edged ridge. He fell into several, but caught himself each time only waist-deep, with the aid of Brad's tight rope. Then the hard crust, so good for crampons, began to give way to a breakable crust with slush beneath. This made for slow going, as the men bruised their shins and cut their socks to tatters on the icy crust.

The men grew as tired as they had been on the summit day on Lucania. "We could not possibly have made it," Brad wrote that evening, "if we had not been able to see the green forests in the distance before we started, and felt that each step was bringing us nearer to warmth and running water."

Yet Bob unerringly chose the right line: not once did the men have to backtrack in the face of an uncrossable crevasse or a vertical cliff. A thousand feet above the base of the ridge, they threw away their crampons, counting on step-kicking slush the rest of the way down. This proved a mistake when, as Bob later wrote, "the slope became steeper, a sort of frozen, windswept scree, with no belays possible." Without packs, the men might have tried a controlled glissade, skiing carefully on the edges of their boots; with sixty-pound loads, such a gambit would have been reckless.

Those last thousand feet proved the hardest and most perilous stretch of the whole descent. Wound to the breaking point with the tension of the treacherous footing, at 8:35 P.M. they stepped at last off Mount Steele. They had completed an extraordinary blind descent of 9,000 feet in only five hours.

After staggering just far enough out to be safe from rocks falling from Steele's slopes, Brad and Bob pitched their tent. At last the weather broke, as a light rain started to fall. But Brad still had the energy for an ebullient diary entry that night: "[W]e are down in God's country again, and for some time there will be nothing but fun!"

He added, "To bed at 10:30, after a grand supper of dried beef, celery soup, gravy, beans, and tea. My, but it's grand to have all the water we need, flowing by us in a real brook. No more melting snow!"

Bob and Brad awoke around 8:00 A.M. on July 12 in the highest of spirits. The rain had stopped. "[W]e had a fine night," Brad wrote in his diary over breakfast. "The sun is shining. Little streams of water are chuckling outside, and all's right with the world!"

The men were off at 9:30. At an altitude of some 7,800 feet, they were lower than they had been at any time during the expedition, and as they hiked along, they basked in the relative warmth. For two hours they traveled roped, until they reached the glacier's snow line, below which only bare ice obtained, leaving the crevasses open and obvious. The head of the Wolf Creek Glacier (known today as Steele Glacier) curls around the skirts of the 16,644-foot mountain, from which it flows first north, then east-northeast, some twenty-three miles toward the lowlands. All Brad and Bob needed to do was follow this broad highway toward the streams that would lead them to their ultimate deliverance at Burwash Landing. Brad felt so good that, observing the curious geology of the region with his professional eye—granite overlying "a weird mass of highly metamorphosed, steeply tilted, reddish rocks"—he planned to add samples to his load as he marched down the glacier.

Nine hours after setting out, the men approached the grassy bench where the glacier bent eastward. They left the ice and climbed the scree of the lateral moraine to gain that shelf. All day they had daydreamed about the bountiful cache Walter Wood had left here; already they could taste the goodies on which they would gorge on the spot and the treats they would add to their packs.

They crested a rise and saw, just ahead of them, metal cans gleaming in the sun. Something was wrong, however. As they came up to the cache, instead of a neatly stacked depot of supplies covered with a tarp, they found cans strewn wantonly in the grass. They picked up several. Each was smashed, with deep holes gouged in the sides. Bob and Brad knew at once what had happened. Sometime during the past two years, a bear or bears had found the cache and destroyed it, biting into every can to get at the exotic-tasting stuff inside. Virtually all the cans had been licked clean, and those that had not been, the men dared not scrape for the residue of food that was left, for fear of botulism. They found only a single intact container—a small jar of Peter Rabbit peanut butter.

"All the way down the ridge," recalls Brad, "we were thinking about what we were going to eat. And we were terribly hungry after that long walk [down the glacier]."

"That was a shock, a real shock," Bob remembers. "Suddenly we realized we were going to run short on food."

In their packs, they now had less than fifteen pounds of food, good for at most four days at the rate they had been eating (and even at that rate, they were constantly famished). There was still the police revolver. With great good luck, they might run across a caribou or even a moose, which, if Bob made a perfect shot with the old gun that fired high and left, they might kill.

As the men stared at the wreckage of the cache, an edge of dread, darker than anything they had felt even during the worst of the storms up on Lucania, seized their spirits. And now a host of doubts and worries about the route ahead, which for twenty-five days they had kept safely tucked in the backs of their minds, thronged to the fore.

F I V E

DONJEK

A T Walter Wood's demolished cache, Brad and Bob were nearing the eastern edge of the collection of aerial photos Brad and Russ Dow had shot in 1935 and 1936. The only map the men possessed rendered the terrain ahead of them a blank (see photo insert). Their knowledge of the lowlands stretching between them and Burwash Landing was based, then, almost entirely on the experience of Wood's 1935 expedition. Their predecessor had published photo-illustrated articles about the first ascent of Mount Steele in both *Life* magazine and *The American Alpine Journal*, and Brad and Bob had consulted him about logistics.

Despite the shock of recovering only a small jar of peanut butter from Wood's cache, Brad, the eternal optimist, wrote in his diary that night, "Walter's horses came up to his base camp; so I imagine our major troubles are over at last." What Brad neglected to mention was an ominous detail. The main obstacle for Wood's team on its approach to Mount Steele had been the Donjek River, a major tributary of the Yukon that flowed from south to north directly across their path. Wood's party had ridden their horses across the Donjek. On the way back out in August, some of the horses had nearly drowned. As Brad and Bob knew well, even the clumsiest horse was a better match for a flooding river than the nimblest man on foot.

The pair had already hiked for ten hours on July 12 before stumbling upon the ruined cache. As if to nip in the bud any plunge in morale their sorry discovery might occasion, they pushed on for another two miles before camping. Brad's diary entry that evening bore only on the positive: "[W]e have a beautiful, almost flat meadow of grass and flowers under the tent. . . . There are plenty of [Dall] sheep, marmots, and birds, and we have seen several bear-tracks but no bear. It is wonderful to hear the birds twitter . . . and realize there is still something alive besides ourselves. How funny it will be to see and hear other people!" The Dall sheep, viewed no doubt from a great distance, might have made a tempting target for Bob's revolver, but among all the wild animals in the Far North, these sure-footed ruminants are the hardest to approach.

It took a while for the novelty of not having to ferry loads across each hard-won stretch of ground to wear off. As Brad wrote that evening, "It's grand to move camp ahead with us as a unit wherever we go, and to realize that each step forward means a step closer to Burwash. . . . To bed on a carpet of flowers—quite a contrast to last night!"

The men's delight in green grass and birdsong and running water and shirtsleeve temperatures was intense. (After spending weeks on high glaciers, climbers in the great ranges are often reduced to tears on regaining the lowlands.) Yet underlying that delight, like the ground bass in a baroque chaconne, was a steady current of anxiety. Reminiscing today, Bob will not quite admit that he felt fear on July 12: "Concern is maybe the better word." A little more frankly, Brad confesses, "We were very worried." The men knew that mid-July marked the apogee of summer snowmelt on the glaciers that fed every river issuing from the Saint Elias Range. On top of that, it had snowed up high (and therefore rained down low) during nearly every one of the previous twenty-five days. If ever the Donjek was likely to be in tumultuous flood, it was now.

On the morning of July 13, Brad wrote, "Our only tools for raft-building are a hunting knife, two packboards, and some rope. But 'necessity is the mother of invention!'" The notion of manufacturing a raft out of driftwood was not as far-fetched as it might have seemed. In 1935, to cross the Alsek River at the end of their monumental traverse of the Yukon icefields, Bob and his two companions had successfully floated a rickety raft made out of skis, air mattresses, and driftwood. But to cross the Donjek in this fashion would be a perilous proposition at best.

Meanwhile, Brad jotted encomiums on the landscape so euphoric that, were he writing today, he might be accused of that trendy psychological syndrome, being "in denial." "What a wonderful morning and what an entrancing spot! There is scarcely a cloud anywhere in the sky. . . . All about the tent the grass is sparkling with dew, and a lovely soft breeze is gently moving the tent. . . . Everywhere the birds are chirping. This is heaven at its best."

Today, Brad and Bob cannot recall whether they carried any cream to prevent sunburn on Lucania (zinc oxide was the only effective ointment of the day). Perhaps not, or perhaps they had run out, for on the morning of July 13, Brad wrote, "We are giving ourselves the Vaseline treatment for our sunburns, which are still quite scaly. We are hoping to come across a brook with a pool or two today, so that we can have a good swim or at least a bath. My dear old suit of [long] underwear was chucked yesterday."

Descending the northeast ridge of Steele, Brad had run out of film. The last photo he had shot was a portrait of Bob probing downward in the lead. Now, on the Wolf Creek Glacier, the Zeiss camera represented dead weight, but Brad could not bring himself to "chuck it out." He was, of course, determined to carry the exposed film that documented the men's adventure back to civilization—and to keep it dry no matter how the men contrived to cross the Donjek. Surrounded by lowland splendor, Brad was grieved not to be able to capture it photographically. "Oh, if we only had some film to get pictures of this wonderful valley!" he wrote in his diary.

Driven by the uncertainty that hung over their fate, and by their dwindling rations, Bob and Brad pushed steadily onward for sixteen hours on July 13, covering as many miles. Even while still on the Wolf Creek Glacier, the men found faint vestiges of the horse trail Walter Wood had blazed up to his 1935 base camp. It was a fine day once again—too fine, for by noon the men were drooping under the overhead sun, which, reflecting off the bare ice across which they strode, assailed them with a double dose of blazing heat. They stopped to eat: "[W]e broke into our loads," wrote Brad later, "and had a fine hot lunch of beans, cheese, and several cups of tea."

As the valley broadened, the men found they could walk along the moraine paralleling the glacier and even, at times, on a tundra bench that formed the right bank of the Wolf Creek drainage. Here, the trail beaten into the vegetation by Walter Wood's thirty-four horses was simple to follow. The hiking was much easier on the bench than on the rubble-strewn glacier, but it came with a drawback. Side streams pouring off the rugged hills that formed the southern rampart of the valley had to be forded. These were surprisingly deep. Brad and Bob waded in with their boots on (the water was too cold, the footing too treacherous to wade barefoot). After each stream crossing, the men stopped, took off their boots, and wrung out their socks. The last ford was the worst, as the water rose to waist-deep and the men felt their legs go numb with cold. The implications were alarming: if these inconsequential sidestreams, draining only a hillside apiece, were waist-deep torrents, what would the Donjek be like?

At 5:15 P.M., Bob and Brad finally passed the snout of the Wolf Creek Glacier, at an altitude of only 4,000 feet. Here, for the first time on the expedition, they found trees—straggling stands of dwarf spruce and willow. The men had been going more than nine hours already, with only a short break for lunch. It would have been a logical time to stop and camp—except that the pair felt the tantalizing pull of another scrap of hope. Harrison Wood—Walter's brother, and one of the four men who had reached the summit of Mount Steele in

1935—had told Bob that about four miles east of the snout of the Wolf Creek Glacier stood a "well-stocked cabin."

At Burwash Landing on Kluane Lake, a French émigré named Gene Jacquot ran a remote trading post. For some two decades, Jacquot had outfitted hunting parties that ranged well to the west, crossing the Donjek on horseback by a ford the guides had worked out over the years. Walter Wood had hired Jacquot's horses and wranglers to get his piles of gear to base camp in 1935. The cabin that Harrison Wood told Bob Bates about was presumably Jacquot's, or that of some forgotten trapper from an even earlier day.

So Brad and Bob pushed on into the evening of July 13. The going was easy, a weary shuffle across an endless level gravel bar interrupted by two or three sidestream crossings. As they hiked, the men paralleled Wolf Creek, a Donjek tributary that flowed out of the glacier the men had spent the last two days descending. Though the creek was several hundred yards to their left, they could hear it "roaring away boisterously."

At 7:00 P.M., Brad and Bob walked off the edge of the easternmost aerial photo in Brad's album. It seemed an appropriate time to stop for dinner. "So we set down our loads and had a good supper of beef, celery soup, and tea," wrote Brad later. "The water was so murky with silt that you could scarcely tell whether the tea had milk in it or not, and the water without soup looked exactly the same as the soup." An hour later, the men hoisted their packs once more and trudged on.

The sun set behind the Saint Elias Range at their backs, and the shadows deepened into semi-dusk. At 9:55 P.M., Brad let out a shout. He had sighted the cabin in the distance ahead. The pair quickened their pace. Reaching the cabin, one of the men seized the front door and opened it.

For the second time in as many days, Bob and Brad were stunned with dismay. The cabin was empty, "except for some old tin cans and a bit of wood," as Brad wrote in his diary—"not even a stove."

Bob recalls that moment: "It was a huge letdown. I'd been in hunters' and trappers' cabins before, and always found a little something, emergency food of some kind. There was absolutely nothing."

Worn to a frazzle, the pair would have used the cabin as a shelter for their camp that night, but they could find no fresh water anywhere near the dilapidated structure. Once more they pushed on into the twilight.

As they moved eastward down the valley, they closed in on the bank of Wolf Creek. Its aspect ratcheted up the men's anxiety by several notches. As Brad wrote that night, "It is all in a single channel and *very swift*. Wolf Creek was the fastest, roughest, and most hazardous glacial torrent I ever hope to see—absolutely uncrossable from start to finish by any means at all."

The men's worst fears about rivers in flood had come to pass. Wolf Creek, only a minor affluent of the Donjek, supplying but a fraction of its volume of silty water, was itself unfordable. The Donjek was likely to be many times worse. The only hope, as Brad and Bob knew from other expeditions, would be to find a place where the Donjek braided into many separate channels, so that the river might be divided and conquered in a series of fords. The men knew further that the best chance of finding such a braided stretch would be to follow the Donjek downstream, in hopes that it began to meander as it entered lower, gentler terrain. But because Wolf Creek itself was uncrossable, and the men found themselves stuck on its south bank, this would not be an option. Any scouting of the Donjek would have to proceed upstream (see map, p. 13).

As the men stumbled on, pushing beyond exhaustion because of the need to know just how things stood, the semi-dusk grew even darker. Sometime after 11:00 P.M., they got another harbinger of bad news. Before they could even see the Donjek, they could hear it—a deep roar of flooding snowmelt, carrying stones and silt with it as it carved its way north.

At last the men arrived. The sight that greeted them was appalling. "The Donjek is a terror," wrote Brad the next morning, "rushing like fury." Even worse than its dizzying speed was the fact that the current, rather than braiding out across the gravel bar, was confined to a single channel backed by the steep hillside across the river to the east. The men decided to camp on the spot. They did not bother to pitch their tent. Wrote Brad, "We are too tired and footsore to do anything but brew some tea, heat some beans, munch a half a pilot cracker each, and 'hit the hay,' sleeping right in the sand and the rocks, with no mattress or anything." Brad had taken a fall in the rocks on the Wolf Creek Glacier sometime that day; now his right knee was sore and stiff. Both men had blisters on their feet, from relentless trudging in wet socks out of which they had been unable to wring all the silt.

Because not only the Donjek but Wolf Creek was uncrossable, Bob and Brad were effectively trapped in the quadrant of lowlands south and west of the junction of those two rivers.

They were still a good thirty-five miles from Burwash Landing. Even eating far less than they wished, they had at most four days' food left. Despite the abundance of animal tracks (that day they had found prints of wolf, moose, and Dall sheep), they had seen no game up close—not even a porcupine. Wrote Brad wryly in the morning, "A magpie and a hermit thrush were the sum total of the live game seen yesterday."

Brad's diary does not indicate how much sleep the men got that night, with such a predicament hanging over them. They were slow to get started in the morning. They had decided at least to investigate the possibility of bulding a raft to cross the Donjek. Near their campsite, they had once more found the old horse trail: that discovery gave the pair hope, for the path ought to lead to the ford that Gene Jacquot's wranglers had worked out. Indeed, at the end of the horse trail, they found the Donjek braided, rather than flooding past in a single channel. The two men started to gather driftwood, but gave up after a few minutes. Without an axe, it would be next to impossible to craft a vessel. Even the subdivided channels, moreover, looked suicidally deep and swift. And, as Brad wrote in his diary, "The river [is] so huge and divided into so many channels that a raft would have to be taken apart and rebuilt a thousand times to get it across."

At noon on July 14, the men sat down to discuss their options. There was really only one possible course. About twelve miles up the river to the south, the Donjek Glacier flowed out of the Saint Elias Range. From their gravel bar, the men could glimpse its dull blue snout in the distance. Their map was useless, and they were well off Brad's easternmost aerial photo, but it seemed obvious that the glacier was the source of the torrential river. What Bob and Brad had to do was hike all the way up to the Donjek Glacier, climb onto its snout, cross the river on the solid ice that gave birth to the stream, then hike thirteen miles back down the Donjek River on the opposite bank to where the horse trail entered the river from the east. "Twenty-five miles to do three hundred yards!" wrote Brad in his diary in disgust.

Whether they were simply worn out from the marathon effort of the previous day, or had begun to weaken from consuming barely adequate provisions, on the morning of the 14th, the men found carrying their sixty-pound loads nearly intolerable. (Both had noticed that they had lost a lot of weight, for their trousers hung loose on their hips.) They decided once more to chuck out some of their baggage—or at least to leave it in a cache, in the forlorn hope of being able to retrieve it in the distant future. To that end, they hung one of the two packboards in a tree near the Donjek, with every last piece of clothing they thought they could do without, and—most agonizing of all—Brad's Zeiss camera and all his exposed film. In that abandonment, there was also a first hint of the pair's darkest thoughts about the upcoming days, for as the men left the cache, Brad said, "Now at least they'll know what happened to us." Bob understood at once: should the two of them vanish in their effort to escape the range, some hunter or mountaineer, perhaps years hence, might come across the cache, retrieve the film, get it developed, and thereby apprehend all but the very end of the story of the first ascent of Mount Lucania.

As they began their march south along the west bank of the Donjek, one man carried a packboard, the other a rucksack. Because the loads were unequal, they traded off every half hour or so. The fuel for their stove was down to a pint of white gas. Their "kitchen" comprised one pot, two cups, one knife, one fork, and two spoons.

At 3:00 P.M., Brad heard a chattering noise in a nearby tree. Veering off course, he spotted a red squirrel scurrying among the branches. Both men dropped their loads, while Bob stealthily unpacked Russ Dow's old police revolver.

Some forty-five years later, Bob recalled the mock-epic hunt that ensued: "I shot—missed. Brad groaned. I went around the tree, shot from the other side, missed. Brad groaned. The third shot, I shot the branch right out from under the squirrel, and he fell down and hit his head. I ran up and grabbed him and finished him off, and Brad said, 'Gee, that was a good shot.' I didn't dare tell him until much later what actually happened."

The men added the squirrel to their rucksack larder and headed on. Soon they came to a mossy glade from which sprouted an abundance of small, light brown mushrooms. They stopped to gather several handsful. Bob remembers the pair's discussion on the spot: "Brad said, 'What do you know about mushrooms?' I said, 'Not very much. I know if there's a death cup you certainly shouldn't eat them.' And I said, 'What do you know?'

"Brad said, 'They say if you cook 'em with a quarter and the silver turns black, they're poisonous. Do you have a quarter?'

"'No.'

"And then Brad said, 'Well, Jim Huscroft [a homesteader the two men had met on the 1933 Crillon expedition] once told me that if you don't eat the brightly colored ones or the white ones, mushrooms in the North are okay.'"

Half an hour later, beside a pretty side stream, the men stopped to cook a late lunch. Into their single pot, they dumped celery soup, a handful of raisins, the stash of mushrooms, and the skinned squirrel. The stew seemed particularly delicious, though Brad commented that the squirrel was so stringy it tasted like piano wire. Afterward, the men lifted their packs and continued south. "As we walked along," Bob recalls, "I would look back at Brad, only to see him turn and look at me. . . ."

The mushrooms proved nonlethal. Six miles from their last night's camp, however—only halfway to the snout of the Donjek Glacier—the men hit a snag they had not anticipated. A stream known to the natives as Spring Creek ran athwart their path. Though it drained a far smaller basin than Wolf Creek, Spring Creek too was glacier-fed, dark with silt, deep, and (in Brad's words) "flowing like the devil." To reach the Donjek Glacier, the men would have to ford this unexpected tributary of the Donjek River.

Fortunately, where the men approached the creek, it was split into eleven channels. They waded into the first, watching uneasily as the current rose to their knees. Almost at once, their legs went numb, and a searing pain, like a bad headache, seized their brains. Shuffling along, feeling with their feet for the underwater stones they could not see through the silt, the men forced their way across one channel after another. The worst one rose waist-deep—the practical limit for men carrying loads in water so swift and cold. On the verge of turning back, Bob and Brad broke through to shallower ground. Spring Creek was behind them.

It was 7:00 P.M. Shivering on the verge of hypothermia, the men took off their trousers, boots, and socks and wrung them as dry as they could. They snacked on a few bites of cheese and "a snatch of raisins" (as Brad called it), and then got back to their feet. Once more, it seemed imperative to push on and resolve the question mark that hung over their lives. The snout of the Donjek Glacier grew nearer by the minute. If they could climb onto it and use it as a heaven-sent bridge, they might by evening reach the east bank of the river—and safety.

At 9:00 P.M., marching along a monotonous gravel bar, the men approached the steep slopes of dirty ice that formed the glacial snout. Across the river they could see small birds flitting among the willows. They could taste deliverance on their tongues.

During the last three days, from the moment when they had stepped off the northeast ridge of Steele to rejoice in running water and green grass, Brad and Bob had felt their exuberant confidence steadily slip away, as a series of setbacks turned what had loomed as a blithe hike to Kluane Lake into an increasingly desperate struggle to survive. The first setback had been the bear-ruined cache on the bend of the Wolf Creek Glacier; the second, the empty hunters' cabin; the third, the uncrossable torrent of Wolf Creek; and the fourth, the raging flood of the Donjek itself. Though they had solved it, even Spring Creek had loomed for about an hour as a fifth setback.

Now Bob and Brad discovered, in the incredulous blink of an eye, the sixth and most crushing setback, and it shocked them into despair. The Donjek Glacier, massive though it was, supplied only a portion, well less than half, of the water that thundered north in the Donjek River. The birds darting among the willows on the far bank mocked the men in their freedom—for what Brad and Bob saw in the near ground was a single cataract of foaming, crashing river. The main course of the Donjek flowed through a stygian canyon, pinched between the rock cliffs of the far shore and the near-vertical ice of the glacier's snout.

Bob and Brad comprehended the sight in an instant. The true source of the Donjek River was not the glacier of the same name. It must be some other glacier upstream to the south—how far, the men could not even guess. (In fact, that source is the Kluane Glacier, its snout a full twenty-two miles away from where the men stood on the gravel bar, staring at their ghastly discovery. With the little food they had left, in the debilitated condition that twenty-seven straight days of extreme exertion had reduced them to, a further march of forty-four miles—to be added to the thirteen more downstream, and the thirty-five that would still separate them from Burwash Landing—was simply beyond their powers.)

In a state that even the perpetually optimistic Brad recorded as "utter dismay," the men threw down their packs, dug out the stove, and brewed up a dreary supper of dried beef, soup, and tea. Then, because there was nothing else to do, they wound their way through mud, bushes, and morainal scree until they had scrambled several hundred feet up onto the snout of the Donjek Glacier. Perhaps, they thought, they could at least get a view up valley to judge just how far away that other glacier, the true source of the Donjek, lay.

But they were too tired to go far. At a quarter before midnight, the two men stopped to camp, leveling out a pitiful platform in the rocks of the moraine between two humps of ice. Having thrown away their tent pole, they used the remaining packboard and their sole ice axe (they had discarded the other up on Wolf Creek Glacier) in a vain effort to prop the drooping roof of the tent a few inches above their noses. "We *swathed* ourselves with the tent," Brad recalls. They struggled into their head-to-toe bivouac in the single, damp sleeping bag, with nothing between it and the ice beneath. They ate a few raisins apiece. To make their bivouac even grimmer, a steady drizzle began to fall.

"That was the worst night of all," Bob remembers. "That was the most miserable and frustrating night I've ever spent in the mountains," adds Brad. "Up till then, we felt as though we were sort of in charge. Now, for the first time, we began to wonder what the hell was going on."

Neither man slept more than a few minutes that night. Too exhausted to discuss their plight, each of them lay in the private cocoon of his fear. For the first time, in fact, true fear overruled the plucky self-confidence that had seen the two men through every previous challenge.

Gazing back on that night's ordeal from the vantage point of sixty-four years of hindsight, Brad summons up a metaphor he borrowed from Andy Taylor, the Klondike veteran, trapper, and mountain man who had been a stalwart member of the 1935 Yukon expedition. "You know the phrase, 'scared shitless'?" asks Brad today. "Well, Andy used to say about his own worst scrape—'The shit was right up in the back of my throat.' That's what Bob and I felt that night."

S I X

RABBIT'S FEET

SHIVERING through the night, Bob and Brad sorely regretted having thrown away their long underwear. They rose at 7:00 in the morning on July 15, played out from lack of sleep. For breakfast they shared two strips of bacon and half a cup of cornmeal mush—the last of their cereal, and nearly the last of their meat. For a day or two, they had been counting their dehydrated baked beans. Now they had only six left, which they decided to save for supper. The rain had stopped, but what Brad called "a wild old southeast wind" rushing down the Donjek valley chilled them to the bone.

Their situation was so desperate that, over breakfast, Brad and Bob briefly discussed the notion of heading all the way back up the Wolf Creek Glacier, reclimbing the 9,000-foot northeast ridge of Steele, crossing the Steele-Lucania ridge at

Shangri-La, descending the 4,000-foot headwall to the Walsh Glacier, retrieving their base camp cache, and stocking up for a hundred-mile hike out to McCarthy. It took only minutes, however, to realize that this was but the wildest of fantasies. If the men lacked the food and energy to hike to the source of the Donjek River and back, they certainly had no hope of reclimbing Mount Steele.

There was nothing to do but push ahead, finish crossing the snout of the Donjek Glacier, and see what lay beyond. For an hour, the men wove their way among piles of talus the glacier had carried down from the highlands through centuries of imperceptible ice flow. Then they came to "a terrible mess of white ice-cracks" (in Brad's words). These were not hidden crevasses covered with thin snow bridges such as the ones Bob had repeatedly fallen into high on Lucania and Steele. The cracks here were bare of snow and thus plain to sight: but they made up a maze of glacial gashes through which the pair had to force a devious route.

Now they regretted another load-saving economy they had performed four days before, when they had abandoned their crampons a thousand feet above the base of Steele's northeast ridge. At the time, neither man had dreamed he would once more face technical ice. Here, in the "mess of white ice-cracks," crampons would have made the going far easier.

Through the worst stretch, a sixty-foot diagonal traverse off a knife-edge of ice, Brad summoned up the technique he had learned as a teenager from the masterly Chamonix guides, as he carved a "downhill staircase" with his axe. (It is much more awkward to chop steps going downhill and sideways than straight up. What was more, Brad had to carve veritable buckets, steps big enough so that the men's sloppy shoepacs didn't slip out of them.)

Just as the two men began to think they were out of the woods, they ran smack into a vertical ice cliff. It dropped away for only twenty feet beneath them, but it was far too steep for chopping steps. They would have to rappel down the cliff.

In the 1930s, to anchor a rappel, a climber normally drove one or more pitons into a crack in the rock, or, on ice, specially designed ice pitons or screws directly into the ice. Brad and Bob had no such gear. The only possible anchor would be a bollard.

The dicey technique of rappelling off a bollard was invented in the Alps around the turn of the twentieth century, before pitons became commonplace. Brad had only read about the dubious technique, which was not one of the pieces of icecraft his Chamonix mentors had taught him in the late 1920s. Now he took his axe and carefully sculpted a ring in the ice near the lip of the cliff—a kind of donut-shaped trench around the fist-sized knob he left in place. When he was done, that knob protruded like an upward-slanting horn. The trick was to hang a doubled rope over this bollard, slide down the rope, which one wrapped in an S-shaped configuration around one's body (all the while praying that the rope didn't slide off the bollard or the bollard itself break), and then retrieve the rope by pulling one end from the bottom.

Now another of the men's load-lightening measures came back to haunt them. On the Wolf Creek Glacier, they had cut up their hundred-foot hemp climbing rope and discarded most of it. The piece they had kept was shorter than the forty-foot length they would need to double over the bollard. So the men resorted to yet another sketchy improvisation, as they untied a piece of flimsy packboard cordage and used it to extend their inadequate hank of hemp. The rappel, though "extremely delicate work," in Brad's phrase, proceeded without a hitch.

After that, the going across the ice became simpler. At 10:30 in the morning Brad and Bob reached the southern edge of the glacier. They could see a walking route off the last of the ice. And for the first time, they could gaze up-valley and gauge where the true head of the Donjek River lay. That distant, blurry snout of the Kluane Glacier was so much farther than the men had hoped, it brought upon their spirits a whole new onslaught of dismay.

Yet in the next moment, dismay was countered by wild hope. Before them, perhaps a hundred feet below, the Donjek River lay braided across more than a mile-wide gravel bar. Staring at that geological apparition, the men counted more than fifty separate channels. A torrent that Brad and Bob had given up all hope of fording might after all be wadable.

So focused on the braids of the Donjek were Brad and Bob, that they almost blundered into a perilous encounter. Just as they scrambled off the last of the glacier ice onto the gravel bar, they spooked a grizzly bear that had ambled near without the men having noticed it. After four days of hiking in which the only game they could scare up was a single red squirrel in a tree, a grizzly was the last thing the men expected (or needed). To their relief, the bear, apparently as startled as they were, took off running instead of charging toward them. As Bob would write in *The Love of Mountains Is Best*, "[H]e was half a mile away before I thought of Russ Dow's police revolver in my pack." In any event, a misaligned pistol would have been a poor match for an aggressive grizzly.

As the men neared the Donjek, the wind blasted their faces with clouds of fine gray dust, blinding them. Then their boots began to sink deep in a sticky brown ooze—quicksand, here in the Yukon where the usual river bank was as hard as a sidewalk. Neither condition boded well for the most dangerous river crossing the men would ever attempt.

It is a curious fact that while more than two centuries of climbing have wrought advances in gear and technique that have revolutionized the art of ascending mountains, in the year 2002 (as in 1937) we know little more about the craft of fording rivers than men did in the Middle Ages. Equipment has done virtually nothing to tame the terrors of flooding streams, especially in the Far North, where glacial temperatures and the ubiquitous silt clouding the water make the task of wading them all the more hazardous.

Each explorer, nonetheless, swears by his favorite method of getting from the near bank to the far shore. Some believe that a pair or trio of waders shuffling along with linked arms makes for a stabler juggernaut. Others insist that the job is best accomplished with a long rope, one wader securing the other from shore; while yet others argue that a rope creates dangers of its own. (An accomplished French climber, Jacques Poincenot, drowned in 1952 in Patagonia crossing a river with a harness hitched to a rope fixed from shore to shore, when one anchor pulled loose and his rig slid down the rope, only to hold him trapped underwater while his teammates tried futilely to release him.) An ice axe propped upstream like a third leg seems to give a modicum of balance to the hapless forder, but it can suddenly swing free in the current and jerk the man off his feet. A few tricks are widely, though not universally, agreed upon. It is probably better to wade diagonally facing upstream rather than straight across, and it is preferable to stare at a fixed object on the far bank rather than the mesmerizing current through which one plows his chilly way. Unfastening the waist belt on one's pack is all but *de rigueur*, for a wader knocked off his feet can be dragged under and drowned by a pack he cannot slip free of as he tumbles with the current. (In Bob and Brad's case, this last point was moot: their packboard and rucksack lacked any semblance of a waist belt.)

As they edged into the Donjek, Brad and Bob had their own theory as to how to maximize their chances. They believed in roping up as far apart as they could get, so they tied all their packboard cordage to their short span of hemp, creating a makeshift seventy-five-foot rope. They added rocks to their fifty-pound loads, in hopes the extra weight would give them added stability. They wore the packboard and rucksack on their backs, but they removed the canvas duffel bags in which their clothing was packed, pulled the drawstrings as tight as possible, and carried these burdens in their arms ahead of them. The idea was that if they lost their footing, the duffel bags might hold air and serve as marginal life preservers.

At 10:45 A.M., as the slightly heavier climber, Bob stepped first into the nearest channel. He crossed it smoothly, and Brad followed. One channel after another succumbed, but patches of quicksand stalled the men: between fords, their legs were caked with gooey brown mud. In a corner of Brad's mind was the realization that all it would take was a single unfordable channel to turn the men back. They would have to reverse each numbing wade, then trudge hopelessly south along the west bank toward the Kluane Glacier, as their last reserves of strength slowly failed them.

After thirty-five minutes of dogged exertion, Brad and Bob had crossed all but two of the fifty-odd channels. As they had seen from the glacier's edge, however, the last two channels promised to be by far the hardest. All the way across, they had dreaded those two deep, fast currents. By now they were on the verge of clinical shock from cold and fatigue. They had said not a word to each other.

In the middle of the first channel, Bob went in over his waist, the deepest yet. All that kept him in balance was the quirk of a locally weaker current. He gained the far bank, then belayed Brad across.

There was only the last channel to go. Brad paid out the rope as Bob waded in. When the full seventy-five feet of line were out, Brad was forced to start wading himself. Near the middle of the channel, Bob went in to his waist, then a little deeper. He staggered, barely in balance, but the current was too swift. Bob fell, dunking his whole body and his pack.

The belay rope gave Bob a second chance. Somehow he got his feet back under him and inched forward. By now, with the rope tight as a clothesline between the men, Brad was waist-deep himself. Then Bob lost his footing once more and started floating downstream. Brad braced to hold his partner, only to have the rope pull him off his stance. The two men began to career out of control down the Donjek, connected by an umbilical cord that promised death, not life.

Yet at that moment, buoyed by the grace of the insouciance with which he met all dangers, Bob surrendered to a technique that was born of pure instinct. The duffel bag he clutched in his hands indeed served to keep his head above water. The current carried him pell-mell for twenty or thirty yards, but then his feet would touch bottom. Rather than try to stand, he hopped, propelling himself forward. Whether in imitation or by kindred instinct, Brad began to float and hop off the bottom himself. Both men today credit the duffel bags with keeping them from going completely under.

At last Bob eddied out on the east bank of the last channel. Gasping for breath, he crawled up to a tundra-covered bench, seized some bushes, pulled himself onto the bench, and collapsed. Brad was only seconds behind. Neither man had the energy to summon up a cheer. "We crossed the goddamn son of a bitch," Brad whispered.

After the men, lying supine in the grass, had caught their breath, they stripped off all their clothes and crawled naked, head to toe, inside their single sleeping bag. Their hands were so numb, they had almost been unable to untie the drawstring of the sack that contained the bag. "I don't know if I've ever been so cold," remembers Bob. For half an hour, the men shivered uncontrollably.

It was too windy to build a fire, but that same wind gradually dried the men's clothes. At last their body heat returned: their teeth stopped chattering and their shivers stilled. Without the sleeping bag, the two would probably have died of hypothermia on the spot. Now, with the returning warmth, a starburst of euphoria and relief bloomed over their midday bivouac.

They were still fifty miles from Burwash Landing, but for the first time, Bob and Brad dared believe that they had solved all the challenges that separated them from civilization. Once they had warmed up, they crawled out of their sleeping bag, put on their almost-dry clothes, ate their last two handsful of raisins, and started hiking north along the Donjek.

After a mile or two, walking along a faint game trail in the tundra, the men scared up another red squirrel. This time Bob nailed it with a single shot. They gathered more of the small brown mushrooms, then stopped to cook a stew of soup and mushrooms, saving the squirrel for the morrow. The meager repast renewed their spirits, so they hoisted their packs once more. Only after retracing eight miles of their long Donjek detour did the men stop to camp. In his diary, Brad recorded: "8:40 P.M. We're laying off early, about four miles north of the end of the Donjek Glacier." "Laying off early," indeed! On July 15, the men had hiked for nearly thirteen hours and survived the closest call of their lives.

Brad's diary entry that evening brims with the joy of the reprieved ("There is moss everywhere—a beautiful fire and scarcely a mosquito") and with his habitual Yankee optimism: "We'll make Burwash now if we have to get through on our hands and knees. My, but it's good to have no hopeless obstacles in the way (except our food is damned scarce). I'd love to make a trip through here sometime with plenty of food and nothing to do but look and sleep and eat. It is such beautiful country that it's a shame to have to miss it all by working under such an awful strain."

In the wake of their deliverance from the Donjek, Bob and Brad enjoyed what the latter called "a prodigious sleep" of more than twelve hours. On the morning of the 16th, while Brad cooked a spartan breakfast, Bob went hunting, but found nothing to shoot. For four miles, they followed the Donjek north, the first two miles on a series of game trails in the trees and tundra, the last stretch on the gravel bar beside the river. At 2:45 P.M. they stopped for a hot lunch: a "mulligan" made up of the stringy squirrel, more mushrooms, half a slice of bacon, one ounce of dried beef, two teaspoons of soup, and their last six baked beans. They cooked this stew on a wood fire, saving their last half-pint of white gas for rainy weather.

So far, Brad and Bob had enjoyed relatively easy traveling in the low country. Yet subarctic taiga—forests of scrubby spruce, birch, and willow carpeted with lush tundra—can be some of the most fiendish terrain on earth to hike across. Because of the permafrost (a layer of ice as little as a few inches below the surface that never melts, even in July or August), the ground often approximates a mossy swamp, through which one wades calf- or even thigh-deep. On drier slopes, sprouting tussocks invite a sprained ankle at every step. Worst of all are the alder thickets, through which one must crawl in a kind of vegetative parody of spelunking, covering as little as a quarter of a mile an hour.

As Bob and Brad tried to follow the Donjek north, the gravel bar gave out, and faint game trails diverted them up into the taiga, where the going indeed grew nasty. The men were sure that when they reached the point opposite where they had first struck the Donjek three days before, a substantial trail—the horse-packing route blazed by Gene Jacquot's wranglers over the years—ought to lead them eastward to

Burwash Landing. Now, as they veered to the right away from the river, cursing each game trail as it petered out in the alders and willows, the men took comfort in the thought that at worst they were striking off on a triangular shortcut that must intersect the Burwash trail. But as the afternoon wore on, there was no sign of that trail. The sky clouded over, and it began to rain. Worn out from their bushwhacking, Bob and Brad entered a zone where high winds had felled hundreds of trees, creating a deadfall maze—a pickup-sticks-like chaos of decomposing timbers—that made the going all the more onerous.

Finally, after 6:00 P.M., they hit the Burwash trail, a virtual highway in the taiga. At exactly that moment, a sizable arctic hare sprang into the clearing. Bob dropped his pack and tore out the police revolver, while Brad tried to fence in the animal. By the time Bob was ready to fire, Brad was dancing, crouched with his hands stretched out, like a basketball player guarding a particularly pesky scorer, with the rabbit directly between them. Afraid that a missed shot might take out his companion rather than the rabbit, Bob tried to signal Brad away, but Brad was oblivious. At last Bob fired, killing the creature with his first shot.

A few miles along the Burwash trail, at 8:45 P.M., Brad and Bob stopped to camp. As Brad wrote, "This diary is about two inches from a big pot of rabbit meat, with ample left for at least one and possibly two more meals; so here goes! We have cut off all four of the rabbit's feet; I'll bet there are no more potent good-luck charms in the world!" The men gorged on three cups apiece of rabbit–mushroom–celery soup stew. Just before turning in, Brad jotted, "The pillow is covered with rabbit's blood, but what do I care!"

Despite that benediction, the men slept poorly, as it rained all night and, jostling each other every time they shifted position in their single bag, they could not get comfortable lying among the tussocks that carpeted their campground. On the morning of July 17—the thirtieth day of their expedition— they did not get off until after 11:00. Before packing up, Brad wrote in his diary, "Two days more of good food; then we'll have to begin to retrench aplenty, unless we kill more game. I certainly hope that we can hold this trail." "Good food" represented Brad's usual optimistic overstatement: the men were down to little more than soup, tea, and the remainder of the rabbit.

There was no escaping the fact that a month of undernourished struggle had taken its toll. Both men were weaker than they had been ten days before, when they had knocked off Lucania and Steele. Loads of only fifty pounds seemed like Sisyphean burdens. Their feet were raw and blistered; their very joints ached. Now, as Brad had feared, they soon lost their trail in the muskeg, the mossy bog underfoot. The rain had stopped, but a steady uphill grade toward the pass that separates the Donjek from the Duke River (a tributary of the Kluane River, which itself merges with the Donjek some fifty miles to the north) slowed their footsteps. They stopped for lunch—more rabbit stew—after less than two hours of hiking. "He was a big snowshoe rabbit, and boy, how good he tastes!" wrote Brad during the break.

After lunch, the men resumed their weary trek. The pass to the Duke River drainage was a mere two miles ahead, so Burwash Landing now lay only some twenty-five miles away. Yet neither Brad nor Bob had any idea what the country was like on the other side of the pass. Might there be other barriers in their path?

Bob recalls what happened next: "We'd been trading the packboard and rucksack back and forth. I happened to be a little ahead of Brad. I heard a sort of clinking sound. I thought, Gosh, that seems strange—we haven't heard anything like that before. I looked back at Brad. He'd heard the clinking sound, too. I looked ahead, and the next thing I saw was a man's hat. It appeared, then disappeared, appeared again, and disappeared again."

The apparition suddenly took on a gestalt in Bob's mind. "By God," he said out loud, "it's a pack horse!"

Brad thought at first that his friend was making a bad joke. Then he saw it, too. Less than two hundred yards away, first one man on horseback rode past, then a second, then a third leading a string of ten riderless horses. As Brad later wrote, "We nearly went crazy with excitement. In fact, I have never been so excited or thrilled or happy all at once in my life."

As startled as Bob and Brad were to run into the first other human beings they had seen in a month, the horsemen were even more so. "Who are you?" one of them managed to blurt out. "Where did you come from?"

Brad waved to the west, saying, "Over those mountains. Where are you going?"

The riders turned out to be two young Indian men, Johnnie Allen and Sam Johnson, and a French wrangler named Paul Bierckel, employees of Gene Jacquot. They were bringing supplies to stock a cabin on this, the eastern side of the Donjek, in preparation for hunters to be guided in August. They also planned to round up some eighteen horses that had been left for weeks to graze on the grassy sandbars of the Donjek.

The five men chatted for several minutes, a bit uneasily, given the strangeness of the meeting. At first Bob and Brad hoped only that the strangers might be able to give them a little food (sugar and coffee were foremost in Brad's mind) and fill them in on the condition of the trail back to Burwash. But when they learned that the wranglers would be returning to Burwash themselves in three or four days, Brad asked, almost timidly, "Would you mind if we joined you?"

Jacquot's men had warmed to the scrawny vagabonds. Within minutes, Bob and Brad were mounted bareback on a pair of horses, while another pair carried the packs they had grown to hate. The string of horses moved slowly northwest, back toward the Donjek. As blissful as it seemed at first to ride rather than walk, Brad and Bob had so little fat on their rear ends that the gentle bouncing became a torture. After about forty-five minutes on horseback, Brad dismounted and walked the rest of the way.

It took the pack train only an hour and a half to reach the cabin. Unlike the one the men had discovered on the other side of the Donjek, this shelter was well stocked. That evening, all five men dined on cinnamon rolls, bread with butter and jam, and roast Dall sheep "that would put filet mignon to shame," as Brad wrote in his diary. (The wranglers had shot the Dall sheep that very day.) Inside the cabin, Brad and Bob laid horse blankets on the floor, spread their tent over them, then used the unzipped sleeping bag as a top blanket. For the first time in two weeks, they had the privilege of stretching out to sleep as they pleased, without worrying that each fidgeting adjustment might disturb the other's repose.

Brad opened his diary entry that evening with a cry of jubilation: *"HURRAH! HURRAH! HURRAH!"* He could not get used to the sudden luxury and safety the chance meeting had guaranteed. "There is enough food in this camp to keep us for a year," he wrote, "and all we have to do now is sleep for the next forty-eight hours. . . . It's superb to hear other people talk; it's grand to take it easy and not worry about how we're going to get over the next pass."

As they spilled out their story to the wranglers, Brad and Bob noticed a certain incredulity on their faces. Two of the men, however, had packed gear up Wolf Creek to Walter Wood's base camp two years before. "[B]oth of them swore they would never set foot in the valley again—a statement with which we both heartily acquiesced!" wrote Brad. The enforced delay while the men rounded up the stray horses seemed a small price to pay for such a deliverance—even to the chronically impatient Brad. "It may be quite easy to round up the horses, or it may take several days," he wrote. "What care we! Our cares and worries are at an end. . . . Lucania and Steele are climbed. The Donjek is crossed, and all our troubles are over."

As it turned out, Brad had gorged on bread and jam and roast sheep so immoderately that he was sick in the middle of the night. Bob's slightly more abstemious intake spared him the same fate. In the morning, an unrepentant Brad shoveled in a breakfast of yet more bread and jam and sheep steaks, and he noted in his diary, "Boy, oh boy, how good that sheep is!" Late the evening before, Johnnie Allen and Paul Bierckel had located the grazing horses; now, on July 18, they went out to round them up. Meanwhile, Bob, who was feeling better than Brad, went out with Sam Johnson to see if they could ford the Donjek on horseback and retrieve the cache in which Bob and Brad had left the camera and all the film.

The horses, along with the Indian wrangler's canny knowledge of the ford, made all the difference. "It wasn't bad," recalls Bob. "The water came up to my knees, but with a good sturdy horse beneath me. . . . We came out on the other side very close to the cache. Sam was as surprised as anything to see it there."

By evening, all the stray horses were staked out near the cabin. Brad was overjoyed at the retrieval of his film and camera. The men spent another night in their palatial shelter. Brad could not bring himself to eat moderately: that night in his diary he sang the praises of "another huge lunch of sheep" and a dinner of "sweet 'tea crackers' and a huge can of sliced peaches, a can of corn, one of tomatoes, and one of peas. . . . I'm so absolutely filled with food of every description that I can scarcely move." "Loafing" all day in the cabin, Brad had composed a newspaper dispatch about the expedition to radio to the East Coast as soon as the men hit Burwash Landing. He had also used a bucket of hot water, soap, and a "clean towel" to wash "over and over again"—his first bath in a month.

It took nine and a half hours on July 19 to cover the thirty miles to Kluane Lake. Brad and Bob rode with only a blanket apiece between them and their wooden pack saddles. Brad would later look back on that ride as one of the worst physical agonies of his life. "We were kind of bony," Bob says. Brad tried for some time to cushion his left thigh by slipping his right hand beneath it, then slipping his left hand under the right thigh, to little avail. At one point, he said to himself, "Christ, I can't take any more of this."

The trek, however, proceeded without incident, though as the horses forded the Duke River, still some six miles from Burwash Landing, Bob and Brad recognized that on foot, they would have had a lot of trouble with this last stream. Since the river was not glacier-fed, however, the water in the Duke was considerably warmer than that of the Donjek.

The pack train reached the trading post at 5:00 P.M. In thirty-two days, counting every load relay, Bob and Brad had covered 156 miles of glacier, mountain, gravel bar, and tundra. Utterly exhausted, Brad managed only two lines in his diary that evening: "Marvelous supper. Too tired, after thirty miles in a pack saddle, to do anything but go to bed *alone*!"

SEVEN

FRESH MILK FROM A REAL COW

A T his trading post on July 19, Gene Jacquot was every bit as surprised as his wranglers had been by the advent of the two emaciated young men who had emerged from the wilderness of the Saint Elias Range. In the best tradition of northern hospitality, nonetheless, he gave Bob and Brad a hero's welcome. By the next morning, Brad had recovered sufficiently to record that reception in his diary. "My, but Kluane Lake looked gorgeous, nestled down among the hills," he wrote, "as we caught our first glimpse of it when coming over the pass out of Burwash Canyon. Best of all, though, was the view of the tidy, neat little cluster of cabins, with its radio masts, as we rounded the little hill above town and walked our horses to the corral."

Brad also managed to expand on the "marvelous supper"

his diary had so laconically documented the night before: "He gave us a supper that would have graced the finest table in Christendom: grayling from the lake, fresh milk from a real cow, mashed potatoes, sheep meat, marmalade, bread, raisin-cinnamon buns, and lemon-meringue pie with delectable crust! Gene used to be a cook or a baker in France before he came here, and he certainly knows his trade." Sixty-three years later, Bob can still taste that dessert. "Yes, lemon meringue pie," he muses, "which Gene personally made just for us."

As delectable as the pie crust was the novelty of the men's first night in bed. Brad and Bob turned in at 8:15 P.M. "In a real spring bed," Brad rhapsodized the next morning, "with a mattress and clean blankets, and a pillow, and pillowcases— all spotlessly clean in a real French style, with a wash basin and clean towels in the neatest, spic-and-span cabin you ever saw in all your life." It rained through the night. "[M]y, how nice it is to hear the lake lapping on the shore and the rain pattering on the roof!"

The radio at Burwash Landing had been established by Pan American Airways to broadcast weather reports to advise their pilots in this mostly uncharted sector of the Yukon (the Alcan Highway, linking Dawson Creek, British Columbia, to Fairbanks, Alaska, would not be built until 1942). Now Brad and Bob used the radio to send cables to their families. The newspaper bulletin that Brad had scribbled down in the Donjek cabin would have to wait till the men arrived in a real town.

The only way in and out of Burwash Landing was by airplane. There was a flight carrying hunters scheduled to arrive from Whitehorse in the Yukon on July 22. Bob and Brad could board the return flight, take the train from Whitehorse to Skagway, then book passage on a pair of boats hopscotching up the Alaskan coast, through Juneau and back to Valdez, where they had left all the belongings they hadn't flown in to the Walsh Glacier with Bob Reeve. On the face of it, two more days of "loafing" under the genial ménage of Gene Jacquot ought to have loomed as a happy prospect.

But Brad, characteristically, was too impatient. When he learned that a Pacific Alaska Airways flight carrying cargo and mail from Whitehorse to Fairbanks would make a stop at Burwash that very day (July 20), he got on the radio to PAA headquarters in Whitehorse. Normally, the airlines had a rule against passengers riding on cargo flights, but the administrator Brad talked to recognized a special case when he heard one. Within five minutes, the climbers had their okay to ride the cargo flight.

By ten that evening, Brad and Bob were lodged in a Fairbanks hotel. "I'm now in a comfortable bed in Fairbanks and Bob is taking a hot bath!" Brad exulted in his diary. A few minutes later, he added, "[H]ere we are, in comfortable warm beds after ice cream, movies, and a pleasant airplane ride!" Bob's memory of that sudden plunge back into civilization, as he wrote of it in *The Love of Mountains Is Best*, betrays a wistful tinge: "It was suddenly over, as if we had just awakened from a dream, but no dream could have made us appreciate so much the luxury of a bed, a chair, and a full meal."

The next day, July 21, these friends, who had been so vitally bound to each other for what would prove to be the most intense month of their lives, parted ways. Bob flew to Anchorage, took a boat south along the Alaskan coast, and eventually rode a train across Canada. (Brad would gather up the belongings Bob had left in Valdez.) A week after the expedition, as he strolled the streets of Montreal while waiting for a train to Boston, still wearing his ragged climbing trousers and his shoepacs, Bob was shocked to see his own face grinning back at him from the front page of the local newspaper. Several columns were given over to an account of the Lucania climb. Brad, still in Alaska, had wired his story east, where it was picked up by the Associated Press and many newspapers, and he had prevailed upon the National Geographic Society, which had sponsored his 1936 aerial photography flights, to release pictures of the climbers and the mountain.

Meanwhile, on July 21 Brad hitchhiked a ride on board a bush pilot's flight to Valdez. Bob Reeve, who must have been vastly relieved to see his young client safe and sound, feigned nonchalance. In Brad's paraphrase, his attitude was "Of course I expected you guys to pull it off. You got back a little faster than I thought you would, that's all." On the spot, the pilot concocted a clever play on names. As Brad recalls, "From that day on, through the rest of his life, Bob Reeve always called me 'Burwash.'"

Brad's intention was to stay another three weeks in Valdez and fly with Reeve to take aerial photos of the Lucania region. He hoped also to persuade Reeve at least to consider a flight in to the Walsh to retrieve as much of the base camp cache as possible, but the pilot made it emphatically clear that he hoped never again in his life to see the Walsh Glacier or Mount Lucania. In the end, Brad stayed in Valdez until August 12, but continued bad weather, along with Reeve's insistence on flying his milk-run mining camp supply drops in preference to serving as Brad's taxi driver, bedeviled his efforts to get new aerial photos of the Saint Elias Range.

As soon as he arrived in Valdez on July 21, Brad reestablished himself in the run-down cabin he had rented for five dollars a month. The first night, it poured rain. Brad woke in the wee hours in the grips of a nightmare. "I dreamed that I was trying to cross a flooding river," he recalls. "I went to the window of the cabin and screamed, 'Help! Help! Help!' There was some guy outside, and he said, 'For Christ's sake, shut up!'"

The newspaper articles made a minor stir. Yet both Brad and Bob remember that when they resumed their jobs that fall—Brad in the Harvard Institute of Geographical Exploration, Bob in the English department of the University of Pennsylvania—their colleagues offered them little more than routine congratulations and showed not a great deal of curiosity about how they had spent their summer.

In the 1930s the American public remained almost completely ignorant of mountaineering. A Boston newspaper, for instance, titled its column-and-a-half story "Cambridge Boy Hero of Climb," but the Associated Press writer had reworked Brad's story into a résumé of the exploit that, at the same time that it made the achievement sound dull and routine, exhibited a thorough incomprehension of what climbing a big mountain was all about. "Roped together to avoid sliding into crevasses, they forced upward"; "Peak after peak rose ahead of them as they climbed through frost and feathers"; "The surface of the glacier proved so badly cracked that Reeve was able to return only after three takeoff attempts"—

such lame approximations betrayed the efforts of the AP hack to grasp the achievement.

Had Brad and Bob been Frenchmen, Italians, Austrians, or Germans who had pulled off a deed in the Alps comparable to their ascent of Lucania, their climb would have made a big splash among a knowledgeable public. Indeed, the following year, when two young Austrians and two young Germans made the first ascent of the Eiger's deadly north face, Adolf Hitler fêted them at a public rally, while the audience wildly cheered the men as Aryan heroes. In America at the same time, mountaineering accomplishments were as obscure as scholarly breakthroughs in entomology.

Brad did his best to dent that ignorance. As soon as he had returned to the East Coast, he took the train to New York and, in typically brash fashion, walked uninvited into the office of Wilson Hicks, a *Life* magazine associate editor, in the Chrysler Building. There he plopped down a copy of *Life*'s second issue of November 30, 1936, featuring Walter Wood's first ascent of Mount Steele. "And so what?" said Hicks.

Brad laid a typescript and a box of eight-by-ten photos on the desk atop the copy of *Life*. "Here's the story," he said, "of the first ascent of your unclimbable mountain." (The final caption of Wood's article, showing a view of Lucania from Steele, had read, it will be recalled, "But Mt. Lucania remains virtually impregnable.")

With the editorial efficiency of the day (an art all but lost in the first decade of the twenty-first century), the September 27, 1937, issue of *Life*—reaching the newsstands scarcely a month after Brad had walked into Hicks's office—ran a handsome eight-page article on Lucania, lavishly illustrated with the excellent photos Brad had captured with his Zeiss camera. The author was Lincoln Barnett, later to make a name as a popular science writer (*The Universe and Dr. Einstein*), working on his first story for the magazine. *Life* paid Brad and Bob a thousand dollars. In one swoop, the men had recovered the cost of the expedition.

With Brad peering over his shoulder, Barnett did a good job. The article was wholly free of the gaffes that had marred the newspaper accounts. "Mountaineering is a compound of sport, science, audacity," the piece opened. "In America it has lately appealed to a growing band of young climbers notable for successes among the peaks of this hemisphere. Less reckless than Bavarians [a backhanded slap at the Eiger candidates, several of whom had died on north face attempts], they have relied on scientific planning, camping ability. Of them none is more precise and competent than Bradford Washburn of Cambridge, Mass."

Yet strangely, the coverage ended high on the northeast ridge of Mount Steele (no doubt because Brad ran out of film there), relegating the climax of the expedition—the desperate hike out to Kluane Lake and the near-fatal ford of the Donjek—to a perfunctory sentence. The article thus presented Brad and Bob's extraordinary traverse and escape as merely a plucky first ascent. Even Bob Reeve's dilemma in the slush, which left the two climbers stranded, was glossed over, its implications unexplained.

Over subsequent years, the Lucania expedition became a legend among the cognoscenti, the peers of Bates and Washburn who themselves sought out first ascents in the remote ranges. Yet Lucania remained off the beaten mountaineering track, seldom visited during the decades after 1937. (Its second ascent did not occur until 1967, when four climbers from California and Colorado flew in to the Chitina Glacier and climbed the mountain from the north. Unlike Brad and Bob, they were also able to fly out.) Thus any detailed knowledge of the dramatic twists and turns of Bob and Brad's journey faded from the memories of all but the most perspicacious students of mountaineering in the Far North. By contrast, a classic route on Mount McKinley, such as the first ascent of the south face by an Italian team led by Ricardo Cassin in 1961, saw its reputation grow more burnished with each subsequent season, for by the late 1980s more than a thousand climbers a year were doing battle with North America's highest peak. Every time a band of young tigers struggled up the Cassin (as the route is nicknamed), they were moved to reflect, "Boy, those Italian guys were ahead of their time." (Allen Steck and Steve Roper's definitive collection, *Fifty Classic Climbs of North America,* includes the Cassin but not Lucania.)

Over the decades, Brad was recurrently tempted to write a book about Lucania, but, busy as he always found himself with the myriad projects that have crowded his professional life, he never got around to it. Bob was content to devote a long chapter to Lucania in *The Love of Mountains Is Best.*

With their friendship cemented for life by their shared ordeal, it would have been logical for Bob and Brad to undertake another expedition together in 1938. This was not to be, however. Only three months after returning from Lucania, Bob got a late-night phone call from Charlie Houston, his Harvard friend and teammate on the 1933 Crillon expedition.

The American Alpine Club had been granted permission to attempt K2, at 28,250 feet the world's second-highest mountain. The club had asked Houston to choose a team. At twenty-five, Houston was at his mountaineering apogee, having pulled off the first ascent of Mount Foraker in Alaska while Brad and Bob were on Lucania. The year before, he had co-led an Anglo-American expedition that had placed two men on top of 25,645-foot Nanda Devi in India—the highest summit climbed anywhere in the world for the next fourteen years, until the French succeeded on Annapurna in 1950.

Houston's first choice for the K2 team was Bob Bates. Today, Bob and Brad cannot recall whether Washburn was invited to K2, but it seems unlikely. Unlike Brad's Alaskan campaigns, K2 was envisioned by the American Alpine Club not as a Harvard- or Ivy League-centered effort, but as a national one. Bates was the only other Harvard alumnus on the team, and the climber who would turn out to be its strongest member was a Wyoming cowboy named Paul Petzoldt, who had made the first ascent of the north face of the Grand Teton. Petzoldt's training, both in school and in the mountains, was as different from that of the HMC gang as could be imagined in 1938.

So Bates spent the summer of 1938 in the heart of the Karakoram Range, then part of the princely state of Jammu and Kashmir, and today within Pakistan. After an arduous and eventful approach march from Srinagar, the team made its way up the Baltoro Glacier to attack K2 by its southeast ridge, a route first attempted by the Duke of the Abruzzi in 1909 (and subsequently named after him). In a brilliant logistical effort, the team strung seven camps up the precipitous

ridge (which is maddeningly short on decent natural tent plat-
forms), the highest at well above 25,000 feet.

Short on time and rations and, vexingly, almost out of
matches with which to light their stoves, the team established
Houston and Petzoldt at Camp VII to make their only try for
the summit. On July 21, that pair gave up at 26,000 feet, Petzoldt climbing a few hundred yards above his exhausted teammate to prospect a line for the future. Theirs was a gallant
defeat, a mere 2,200 feet below the top: K2 would not be
climbed until 1954.

Meanwhile Brad spent the summer of 1938 in Alaska. It
turned out to be one of his finest seasons in the mountains,
for, in clockwork fashion, his teams made the first ascents of
13,176-foot Mount Marcus Baker, the highest peak in the
little-explored Chugach Range east of Anchorage, and of
16,237-foot Mount Sanford in the Wrangell-Saint Elias
wilderness. On Marcus Baker, undaunted by his near-disaster
on the Walsh Glacier, Bob Reeve once more flew Brad's party
in, this time making a series of successful landings at 5,000
feet on the Matanuska Glacier.

On July 9, 1937, Mount Sanford had become the new highest unclimbed peak in North America. A sprawling glaciated
mountain like Lucania, it is far more accessible: on the very
western edge of its range, Sanford lords its lofty summit over
the Glenn and Richardson Highways, which connect the
towns of Tok and Glennallen and Valdez. Brad's approach to
this new challenge was something of a throwback to the pioneer days, as he and Harvard crony Terris Moore (who had
been on the first ascent of Fairweather in 1931) horse-packed
in to the mountain's base, mushed a dog team to a 10,000-foot

advance camp, strolled to the summit, then skied all the way down in one glorious 6,000-foot run.

In view of their near-perfect friendship, there is a slightly rueful irony in the fact that after Lucania, Bob and Brad would share only a single other expedition. That came in 1942, when, with the country newly at war, the Army Air Corps and the Office of the Quartermaster General collaborated with the American Alpine Club to put a large team on Mount McKinley's Muldrow Glacier. The rather ponderously named U.S. Army Alaskan Test Expedition had as its rationale field-testing cold weather gear in extreme conditions. Among its seventeen members were not only Brad and Bob, but Terris Moore and Walter Wood.

The expedition indeed performed a great deal of valuable testing of equipment, which would later pay its dividends in the Tenth Mountain Division's campaign in Italy. For Brad and Bob, however, this was also a chance to bag the third ascent of McKinley. They succeeded, with two teammates, on July 23, in glorious weather, after a night during which the temperature dropped to minus 23°F. The Test Expedition, however, with its cadres of specialists (dog mushers, scientists, and a cook, as well as climbers), with massive support in the form of supplies air-dropped in by parachute, stood as the antithesis of the fast-and-light style Brad and Bob had perfected on Lucania.

Nor, among the tent colonies of a seventeen-man expedition, was there any vestige of the intense intimacy that had welded Brad and Bob together five years before in the Saint Elias Range. It is ironic that on summit day, Bob and Brad were roped not to each other, but to other partners, Bob with

Terris Moore, Brad with a climber from California named Einar Nilsson.

In 1939, as he pursued grad-school work at Penn toward his dissertation on the English writer and antiquarian John Aubrey, Bob was surprised to be offered a job teaching English at his former prep school, Phillips Exeter Academy. With minor interruptions for World War II and other service abroad, Bob would teach at Exeter for thirty-seven years, until his retirement in 1976. Legions of students, many of whom became first-rate climbers themselves, fell under the spell of Bob's gentle pedagogy in the classroom.

The same year that Bob took the Exeter job, Brad accepted the offer that would shape his own professional life, as he was appointed director of the New England Museum of Natural History. At twenty-eight, he became the youngest director of a major museum in the country. During the next forty-one years, Brad turned the ramshackle and moribund New England Museum into the Boston Museum of Science, one of the leading institutions of its kind in the world.

Among his first acts at the New England Museum was to fire what Brad recalls as "a battle-axe of a secretary" and replace her with fresh blood. One candidate recommended by an acquaintance was Barbara Polk, a good-looking, twenty-four-year-old Smith College graduate then working as a secretary in the Harvard biology department. Barbara's initial reaction to the lead was not auspicious. "I don't want any part of that guy Washburn," she told the friend who had recommended her. "The last thing I want is to work for a crazy mountain climber in a stuffy museum."

The friend pushed her into a trial interview, which got off

to a dismal start. As a child, Barbara had been taken to the New England Museum by her parents. Her strongest memory of the place was of a whale skeleton, covered with dust, hanging from the ceiling. Barbara double-parked her car outside, so sure was she of a quick termination to the interview. "My heart sank as I entered the museum," she wrote in 2001, looking back on that long-ago day. "It seemed even more depressing than I remembered."

The twenty-eight-year-old director's bearing upset her expectations: "He was rather slight, had no beard, and bore no resemblance to the pictures of explorers I had seen in picture books, pictures of men like Lewis and Clark." Brad at once started talking about finances. Anxious to reclaim her double-parked car, Barbara snapped, "I don't know anything about finances."

"But you can learn, can't you?" Brad countered. Barbara took the job. She and Brad were married on April 27, 1940.

Though Barbara had little experience in the outdoors, Brad insisted at once on taking her along on his Alaskan expeditions. She proved a natural adept, reaching the summit on the first ascents of 10,182-foot Mount Bertha, in the Fairweather Range, in 1940, and of 13,740-foot Mount Hayes, the highest peak in the Hayes Range in central Alaska, the following year. Both climbs were actually technically more difficult than Lucania. The capstone of Barbara's mountaineering career came in 1947 when, against her own better judgment, she left her three young children in care of both sets of grandparents to join Brad on a three-month expedition to Mount McKinley, where he made his second ascent and she became the first woman ever to stand on the top of the North American continent.

In 2001, Barbara published a memoir of her life with Brad, disarmingly titled *The Accidental Adventurer*. Not surprisingly, her vignettes of her husband at work and play in the mountains characterize him more pithily than anything Brad ever wrote for *The American Alpine Journal*. In a dicey moment on McKinley, for instance, as Barbara and Brad struggle to down-climb a steep ice pitch as a storm gathers,

> Brad jerked the rope and shouted to me, "You've simply got to move faster. The storm is approaching rapidly."
>
> I looked at him, fifteen feet away, and said calmly, "I am the mother of three small children and I've got to get down from here safely."
>
> He replied immediately, "Don't forget, I'm the father of those small children and I want to get down safely, too."

For more than two decades, from 1930 to 1951, Brad led expeditions to Alaska and the Yukon approximately every other year. His first three ventures, on Fairweather in 1930 and on Crillon in 1932 and 1933, had been failures, in the sense that his teams were stopped short of the summit. From 1934 on, however, not once did Washburn attempt a climb in the Far North without reaching the top. In the process, he racked up a roster of first ascents that stands as the most dazzling record of any mountaineer campaigning in Alaska and the Yukon.

It is significant that Brad never climbed in the Himalaya or the Andes. Once he had focused on the North American sub-arctic, he had found his life's work as an adventurer. Brad's swan song came in 1951, at the age of forty-one, when he led a two-pronged assault on the unclimbed West Buttress of McKinley—a route he had discovered from his own aerial photographs. Presciently, Brad predicted that the West Buttress would turn out to be the easiest route on the mountain. Today, it is the *voie normale,* thronged yearly with 90 percent of the thousand-plus alpinists who set out to add Denali to their trophy lists (only half of whom succeed).

After 1951, Brad ceased to lead major expeditions in quest of first ascents. But his passion for aerial photography in Alaska and the Yukon only intensified. At first, that passion had amounted to a pragmatic hobby, as Brad sought (as he did in scouting Lucania in 1935) to bring back pictures that would help him plot his own future ascents. Soon, however, the effort became an end in itself. Thanks to his own perfectionism—he insisted on flying with the airplane door removed, his body roped to the fuselage as he leaned out, swaddled against the wind and cold, cradling in his lap a large-format camera that weighed some fifty pounds—the photos attained the quality of true art.

It was not Brad, but others, who first recognized the worth of his oeuvre as art. Well into the 1970s, Brad sold his pictures to climbers (for whom that collection had become a gold mine of new-route possibilities) at the cost of printing them. Today, his photos fetch high prices at auctions, and in the 1990s he was invited to mount one-man exhibitions at the prestigious International Center of Photography in New York and at Boston's Museum of Fine Arts. In 1983, Ansel Adams hailed Brad's achievement, writing, "[T]he photographs look almost inevitable, perfectly composed. These are not simply documents . . . ; we sense in each one the presence of an individual, highly intelligent eye. The photographs are the result of the explorer's consistent energy of mind and spirit—and so they truly *mean* something."

Among his other accomplishments, Brad became an innovative cartographer. His maps of Denali and Everest, produced in conjunction with the Swiss Foundation for Alpine Research and the National Geographic Society, are perhaps the most exquisite mountain charts ever made. Brad's fascination with Everest had been sparked way back in 1926, when Captain John Noel had lectured at Groton on the fateful Mallory-Irvine expedition of two years before. Though Brad has never even hiked to Everest base camp, in the 1980s he began coordinating stereo photography of the world's highest mountain from the air, and he persuaded young climbers to carry GPS surveying equipment to its summit, which, coordinated with Brad's measurements from the lowlands, produced the beguiling result in 1999 that Everest was seven feet higher than everyone had thought it was for most of the century.

Not many people realize that in the 1930s, Brad also became a first-rate small-plane pilot. His skills in the cockpit were so highly thought of that, in January 1937, Brad was invited to a soirée at the home of his erstwhile publisher, George Palmer Putnam, and his wife, Amelia Earhart. The pair wanted Brad's advice about the feasibility of what was still a secret project—Earhart's attempt to fly a Lockheed Electra around the world. Implicit in the meeting was a possible invitation to Brad to serve as Earhart's navigator.

Brad surveyed the charts and plans, fingered the crucial weakness in them, and bluntly told Putnam and Earhart what he thought. On the next-to-last leg, it would be crazy to take off from New Guinea and try to hit Howland Island in the mid-Pacific, a needle in the haystack, by dead reckoning. On the other hand, if Earhart took the trouble to get a ship to stop at Howland beforehand and install a radio transmitter sending out a signal that Earhart could pick up from her plane, the scheme might work.

Impatient with such details, Earhart ignored Brad's advice. Heading for Howland Island, 2,550 miles away, she took off from Lae, New Guinea, on the evening of July 1, 1937—eight days before Brad and Bob would stand atop Mount Lucania—with Fred Noonan as her navigator instead of Brad. She intended to fly through the night and land on the tiny island in the morning. Her last radio call was heard by a ship near Howland at 8:45 A.M. on July 2.

At the age of 92, Brad is a minor celebrity, with a string of medals and honors (the Lowell Thomas Award of the Explorers Club, the Discovery Lifetime Award of the Royal Geographical Society, the National Geographic Centennial Award, honorary doctorates from Harvard and Boston University, etc.) the likes of which, were he British, would probably earn him a knighthood. Looking back on his career, Brad often says that his proudest achievement is the founding and directing of the Museum of Science. Mountaineers, however, will always hail Brad's climbing and exploration, buttressed by his six decades of mountain photography, as the reason history will remember the man.

Bob Bates did not marry until 1954, at the age of forty-three. He had met Gail Oberlin, the sister of a climbing friend, a few years before, at an American Alpine Club meeting in Philadelphia (she was the club's secretary). Gail had climbed in the Alps long before she met Bob. After their marriage, they shared many a far-flung exploratory trek together, to the Ojos del Salado on the Chile-Argentina border, to Iceland, to Sikkim in India and Bhutan, and to the Ruwenzori Mountains of Uganda, among other destinations.

With his 1938 K2 expedition, Bob had ventured for the first time beyond the realm of Brad's favorite ranges in Alaska and the Yukon. Though he would climb again in the Far North, Bob was interested in mountains all over the world. Nor did he give up serious climbing in his early forties, as Brad did. In 1966, at the age of fifty-five, Bob teamed up with H. Adams Carter, a Harvard pal three years his junior (and a veteran of the 1933 Crillon expedition), and the legendary British climber Eric Shipton, who was fifty-nine, for an attempt on a new route on Mount Russell, southwest of McKinley. A vicious storm shredded the men's tents and forced them to make a grim retreat just to save their lives. As late as 1985, at the age of seventy-four, Bob joined a Chinese-American team that made an arduous trek into little-known Xinjiang Uygur region of China to reconnoiter a major unclimbed mountain, 22,917-foot Ulugh Muztagh.

Ensconced at Exeter, Bob has led a professional life far less public than Brad's—as befits his modest nature. He did serve as president of the American Alpine Club (today he is the club's honorary president), and as the first director of the Peace Corps in Nepal from 1962 to 1963, work he found, with his limitless curiosity about other cultures, both fascinating and, in the end, frustrating. (In Kathmandu, Gail developed a mysterious illness and lost thirty-five pounds before returning to the United States.)

It was in 1953 that Bob underwent the single mountaineering tragedy of his life—as well as, with Lucania, one of his two closest calls. Though they were forty-two and forty years old respectively, Bob and Charlie Houston decided to mount their second attempt on K2. They put together a strong team of younger climbers from all over the country. As they headed off to Pakistan, Bob and Charlie had every expectation that this time they would reach the top of the world's second-highest mountain. After a hiatus during World War II and the four years following, when no Himalayan expeditions entered the field, the fourteen peaks in the world higher than 8,000 meters (about 26,247 feet) were starting to fall, beginning with Annapurna in 1950. Everest itself would be climbed in 1953 by Hillary and Tenzing, and Nanga Parbat in a unique solo summit push by the fanatical and gifted Austrian Hermann Buhl.

High on the Abruzzi Ridge on K2, however, team member Art Gilkey, a Columbia University geologist and Teton guide, suddenly developed an ailment that so crippled him he could not walk. Houston, a doctor, diagnosed thrombophlebitis, caused by a blood clot in the leg. Instead of going for the summit, the whole team had to bend its efforts to saving Gilkey's life, lowering him, swathed in a sleeping bag, with ropes. On the technical terrain of the sharp ridge, this proved a nearly impossible task, forcing the men to take risks they would normally never have countenanced.

On August 10, disaster struck. As the team descended in roped pairs, one man slipped and fell; the rope dragged his partner off his feet. Their rope tangled with Bob and Charlie's, pulling them in turn from their footsteps: suddenly four men were sliding out of control toward the void. Highest on the slope, a Seattle stalwart named Pete Schoening had paused to anchor the helpless Gilkey, while a seventh team member, also roped to Gilkey, probed ahead. The falling ropes yanked this man too from his stance. It seemed inevitable that seven men would plunge, linked by their tangled ropes, to their deaths off the Abruzzi Ridge.

Schoening thrust his axe into the slope uphill from a large rock, leaned on it, and hung on for dear life. In what is still known nearly half a century later as "Schoening's miracle belay," he held the shock, which came not all at once, but in a series of jolts, as the ropes that had pulled the men from their feet now served to stop their falls one by one.

Several team members were injured and frostbitten. Houston was in shock, delirious and disoriented, barely comprehending which mountain he was on. The less injured teammates worked into the night getting tents pitched on precarious perches and their friends into their sleeping bags. Meanwhile, the men left Gilkey tied off to an anchoring ice axe, only a hundred yards away.

In the midst of their frantic toil, an avalanche they failed to hear scoured the nearby slope. When Bob and two others climbed back to get Gilkey, they were shocked to see nothing but bare ice. The avalanche had swept their teammate, anchoring ice axe and rope with him, off the mountain. (Gilkey's body was not found until 1993, when a party stumbled across his skeleton below the Abruzzi Ridge, carried by the glacier's flow during those thirty-nine years four miles from where he had fallen.)

Though none of the survivors could acknowledge as much at the time, Gilkey's death came not only as a tragedy but as a deliverance. It was all the other men could do to get them-selves down the ridge and back to base camp. The book Bates and Houston wrote about the expedition, *K2: The Savage Mountain,* has become a mountaineering classic.

H A D Brad and Bob drowned in the Donjek in 1937, they would be remembered today—though perhaps only dimly, like Allen Carpé, who vanished in the crevasse on the Muldrow Glacier at the zenith of his Alaska career—as mete-oric martyrs to an indifferent wilderness. Their coevals might recall them as the brightest of their generation of northern mountaineers, their lives snubbed out by the whim of a flood-ing river at the denouement of their finest climb. It is even possible that no one would have ever known what Brad and Bob accomplished on Lucania and Steele. Their bodies would almost certainly never have been found. They had left nothing on the summit of either mountain to record their passage. The chances would seem relatively slim that some other mountaineering party, twenty or forty years later, might climb Steele's northeast ridge and discover, not yet buried under the snows of the decades, the crampons or the snowshoes or the tent pole the men had discarded on their descent.

Perhaps knowledge of Brad and Bob's achievement would have hinged on the discovery by some lowland party—maybe Jacquot's wranglers—of the cache the pair left in the tree on the west bank of the Donjek. Such a party would have had to recognize the significance of the find, without suspecting that any mountaineers had entered that wilderness since Walter Wood in 1935. Before such a discovery could have been made, on the other hand, bears might have torn the cache to pieces, strewing its contents on the gravel bar, smashing the camera and spoiling Brad's rolls of exposed film.

Instead, both Brad and Bob not only survived all their expeditions, but lived long enough to mellow gracefully into their tenth decades. It is hard not to envy the men's quiet pride in their lifetimes of achievement in and out of the mountains. Both have been blessed with long-lasting marriages that were also true partnerships. And both readily admit that what has anchored their lives is an abundance of enduring, unquestioned friendships, of the sort about which Homer sang. (As Brad is fond of joking, much to his wife's chagrin, "I've always said the only two good bed partners I've ever had were Barbara and Bob Bates.") The two men still visit each other regularly, as they did one frosty day in January 2001, to celebrate Bob's ninetieth birthday.

From the armchair in the living room of his retirement-community apartment in Exeter, New Hampshire, Bob radiates an unmistakable serenity. His zest for life undimmed, he still travels with Gail to the corners of the globe. If *The Love of Mountains Is Best* rings today as a bland, old-fashioned motto, it nonetheless serves as the appropriate epigraph for Bob's life.

Less serene, impatient as ever in his ninety-second year, Brad still works every day out of a home office in his own retirement-community apartment in Lexington, Massachusetts. Anticipating the years to come, he bluntly remarks, "I hope and pray I just drop dead of a whopping heart attack."

It is not far-fetched to see Brad's and Bob's most dangerous expeditions as keys to their longevity and fulfillment. From

Lucania, they brought back not only the triumph of a first ascent, but the kind of momentary renewal of the world that the best adventures can work, turning something as mundane as "fresh milk from a real cow" into a sacrament suffused with wonder.

In the light of the history of mountaineering, it was certainly not technical difficulty that made the first ascent of Lucania such a benchmark. Bob and Brad faced not a single move of rock climbing on their month-long expedition, and their hardest work on snow and ice amounted to chopping steps up steep slopes and crossing thinly bridged crevasses. On K2 in both 1938 and 1953, Bob climbed much more difficult pitches than anything on Lucania, as did Brad on Mount Hayes in 1941 or, for that matter, on the Aiguille Verte in 1929.

On Lucania, it was the collision of the risky new gambit of using a ski-equipped plane to approach a remote mountain with some of the weirdest weather either Brad or Bob Reeve would ever see in the North that led to the men's dramatic dilemma—two climbers marooned in an uncharted wilderness, a hundred miles from the nearest other human beings, left to their own devices. What stamps the 1937 adventure with its special genius is the boldness with which Brad and Bob responded to that near-catastrophe. In the shape of their lives, as confident as climbers have ever been in the great ranges, they escaped their captivity by accomplishing what they had come to the Yukon to do: get up the highest unclimbed mountain in North America. What did it matter that the way out lay across a blank in the map, a blank that they nonetheless knew before they started was bisected by a river that would give them all the trouble they could ask for?

In the end, Bob and Brad pulled it off by inches—but those inches were the measurements by which they had built their doctrine of fast and light. Sixty-four years later, we can look back and say that in the history of mountaineering, there is no other deed quite comparable to Brad and Bob's in 1937. And in our own modern age, with exploration abetted by helicopter rescues and global positioning systems and satellite phones, with no true blanks left anywhere on the map of the world, another Lucania will never again come to pass.

EPILOGUE

IN February 2001, I finished the last of several marathon sessions of tape-recording Bob and Brad's reminiscences about Lucania and about their lives before and after. I guessed that I knew the story of that extraordinary climb as well as anyone could who hadn't even been born in 1937. Thanks to Brad's superb photographs and to modern maps, I felt that I knew my way around Lucania.

Yet something nagged at me. Although I had pursued thirteen mountaineering expeditions of my own to Alaska and the Yukon in the 1960s and 1970s, I had never climbed in the Saint Elias Range. Driving the Alaska and Glenn Highways, I had admired the northern and western ramparts of that great sprawl of glaciated peaks. But I had never seen Mount Lucania, not even from an airplane.

When Brad mentioned that he was being flown up to Denali National Park in July for a celebration of the fiftieth anniversary of his first ascent of the West Buttress, an obvious plan was hatched. Once the park rangers were finished fêting Brad, could we not hire a bush pilot and fly over the Saint Elias Range, retracing by air the route of his Lucania expedition sixty-four years after the fact? Brad was all for it.

I met Brad and Barbara in Anchorage on July 14. Art Davidson, an old climbing buddy of mine and one of the three men who had made the first winter ascent of McKinley in 1967 (and nearly died in the process), hosted a crab fest at the sylvan homestead he had built south of town in Rainbow Valley. A small throng, comprising some of the best Alaskan mountaineers of the second, third, and fourth generations after Brad's, paid homage to both him and Barbara. Kneeling on the grass in Art's front yard, they peered over Brad's shoulder as he unrolled the exquisitely detailed Canadian government quadrangles and, with the back end of a ballpoint pen, retraced the route of his escape from Lucania.

The next morning, Brad, Barbara, and I drove out of Anchorage in a rental car. The weather had been lousy, Art had told me, for two solid weeks, and now it was overcast and raining. I had lined up a bush pilot, but now, as we crept northeast on the Glenn Highway, I contemplated the glum prospect that we might arrive in McCarthy only to cool our heels, using up our few available days while Lucania sat, invisible and unflyable, smothered by the storms that, after all, were business as usual for a range so glaciated as the Saint Elias.

As we passed through Palmer, though, the rain stopped

and the clouds started to break up. By the time we had climbed up the canyon of the Matanuska Valley, patches of blue sky were showing in the east. Brad peered intently out the righthand window. All at once the bluish snout of the Matanuska Glacier appeared between steep ridges cloaked with spruce and fir. Some twenty miles up that glacier, Bob Reeve had landed Brad's party in 1938, when they had made the first ascent of Mount Marcus Baker.

"If Reeve couldn't fly back in to pick us up," Brad said now, "we had a plan. We were going to hike down the Matanuska Glacier, build a raft out of driftwood, and float out to Palmer." In 1938, the Glenn Highway had yet to be built, and this gloomy canyon was uninhabited. Brad stared at the chaos of morainal debris and braided river below us on the right. "We'd have never made it," he said softly. "They'd have never found us."

Just past Eureka, the highway bursts out of its claustrophobic gorge to traverse a gloriously green tundra plateau. The sun had burst upon us as well. We stopped to take some photos. All around us, magenta fireweed blazed in riotous bloom, and mosquitoes swarmed.

It is possible to drive to McCarthy, but the last sixty miles from Chitina proceed along an unpaved old railroad bed that is so littered with rusty spikes and nails that you can count on a flat tire or two. (The rental car companies forbid this passage, but in anarchic Alaska no one pays attention to such fussy rules.) I had arranged instead for our pilot to pick us up at Glennallen and fly us in to McCarthy.

The outfit I had hired was Wrangell Mountain Air, run by Natalie and Kelly Bay. At 8:15 P.M., with the slanting late-afternoon sunlight bathing the tundra, a yellow-and-white Cessna 206 put down on the dirt strip at Glennallen. As we loaded our luggage aboard, Barbara said, "Plenty of room." "It's our station wagon," answered Natalie Bay. An Aussie by birth and accent, she had come to Alaska in 1983, fallen in love with the place and with her soon-to-be husband, and stayed for good.

Brad got into the co-pilot's seat, with Barbara and me in the seats behind. All at once we were in the air, gliding over the taiga skirts of the Wrangell Mountains. Brad's old pilot instincts came to the fore. "There's no rudder on the co-pilot's side," he complained into his headphone. Natalie glanced at him and smiled, "But you've got everything else." Realizing that she had an aviator beside her, she asked Brad in what craft he had learned to fly.

"I took my first flights," he answered, enunciating as if to a schoolchild, "in a Kinner Fleet biplane. I'll bet you've never seen one of those." Natalie allowed that she hadn't.

The air was utterly smooth. On our left, one by one, the isolated hulks of Mounts Drum, Sanford, Wrangell, and Blackburn, dormant volcanoes covered with massive glaciers, crept by. Brad peered at Sanford, tracing a line in the air to show us where he and Terris Moore had skied down from the summit in 1938.

We crossed a low divide and suddenly found ourselves in the Chitina valley. Circling over the Kennicott Glacier, we came in to land on the 3,500-foot dirt strip at McCarthy. We were only forty-five minutes out of Glennallen.

Although McCarthy had been crucial to the 1937 expedition—for it was from this strip, then covered with snow, that

Bob Reeve and Russ Dow had flown in the depot of base camp supplies to the Walsh Glacier in May—Brad had never before visited the town. A Wrangell Mountain Air employee drove us four miles up a hillside to the Kennicott Lodge.

The wooden hotel, painted dark red with white trim, was designed to match the spectacularly derelict Kennecott Mine complex beside it. (Though named after Robert Kennicott, an early U.S. Geological Survey explorer, the mine had been founded in 1906 by men who managed to misspell his name.) The lodge and the mine gaze out over one of the most sublime settings in Alaska, with the talus-covered jumble of the Kennicott Glacier below in the foreground, and beyond, a lordly vista south across the basin of the Chitina valley, here at its broadest, a good fifteen miles across. We spent two nights in this comfy (if overpriced) hotel, sharing the hearty family-style meals served up for the tourists whom the all-too-brief summer lures to this outback of pioneer Alaska.

Brad knew that Andy Taylor, the Klondike veteran who had taught him so much about winter camping and dog mushing on the 1935 Yukon expedition, had spent his last years in McCarthy. We made our way down to the old town below, a scattering of dwellings nestled among the birch trees, and, after inquiring of oldtimers, found the trim miner's cabin, now boarded up, that had been Taylor's last residence. Brad took a picture of the house.

At eight in the morning on July 16, we met Kelly Bay at the airstrip as he gassed up a spiffy yellow-and-red Cessna 185. The weather was holding magnificently. "You folks are in luck," said Kelly. "Best day so far of the whole summer." We climbed into this smaller plane, the craft of preference for bush flying in the North. Brad once more took the co-pilot's seat; Barbara sat directly behind him, while I sat on the left behind the pilot.

A big, rangy, affable fellow with a dark black beard sprinkled with gray, Kelly filled us in on his background as we gained height and swung southeast toward the main Chitina valley. He had come to Alaska in 1975 from his native Seattle, a young man looking aimlessly for adventure. "Did a lot of trapping with dogs in this country," he said into his headphone, "marten, wolverine, lynx, the occasional wolf. I took up flying when I got tired of looking at the wrong end of a dog. Did some trapping with a snow machine, but there wasn't any fun in it."

In 1980, the Wrangell-Saint Elias National Park and Preserve was established, putting an end to the big-game hunting that had been the chief draw for visitors to McCarthy through the 1960s and 1970s. During those last pre-park years, Kelly admitted with a guffaw, he had done some "unauthorized" flying of Dall sheep hunters (he had had as yet no bush pilot license)—"mostly friends, for pocket cash," he added. "Then I figured, why not start an air taxi?"

Brad told Kelly about our discovery of Andy Taylor's house. Taylor had been dead so long that he seemed to locals a figure out of ancient myth. "Did you know Andy Taylor?" Kelly asked, incredulous.

The Chitina River was directly under us, maybe 2,000 feet below. I stared at the wide meanders of its chocolate-colored current, the same meanders Brad and Bob had apprehensively surveyed on their way in with Reeve, with the sky getting darker and darker ahead. Here, at least, I thought, the walking would not have been terribly arduous, on the fringe where the forest met the gravel bar.

"What was Bob Reeve like?" asked Kelly.

"He was a man of few words," said Brad. He retold the story of Reeve's telegram, "ANYWHERE YOU'LL RIDE, I'LL FLY," then added a footnote: "He rescinded the whole thing afterwards."

As we flew, Brad whistled softly and tunelessly into his headphone, a kind of nervous tic he had adopted, I had noticed, during the last decade. Still gaining altitude, we passed over the snout of the Chitina Glacier. I craned my neck to look down at it. Here was "that nauseating desolation of dying masses of ice," those "potholes full of horrid muddy water fill[ing] every depression in the hellish sea of stagnant ice" that Brad had noted in his diary on June 19, 1937. The glacial snout indeed looked like nasty going, but in the sunshine and calm air, everything in this gleaming wilderness seemed to take on a benign aspect. On either side, unnamed mountains rose to 8,000 feet, each promising a major challenge in its own right.

Where the Chitina branched from the Logan Glacier, we followed the latter. Here we were over the route of the epochal pack-in on the first ascent of Mount Logan in 1925. Brad was taking color slides with his Nikon, mere snapshots compared to the large-format black-and-whites he had spent six decades fine-tuning; but with a series of impatient hand signals, he directed Kelly Bay to dip his left wing or fly in a half circle so he could get the shot he wanted. When he was ready, he opened the small window, careful to ease it upright so that it didn't snap in the sudden airflow, in order to shoot through transparent space rather than scratchy Plexiglas. Each time he opened the window, an arctic blast struck Barbara in the face. She balled up a big down jacket and held it in front of her for protection.

Brad was awash in 1937 memories. "It was around here," he told us through his headphone, "that Bob Reeve said, 'Look, if we go any farther, we have to stop and refuel.'" Then, as we glided steadily up the Logan Glacier, Brad suddenly remembered his first view ever of this terrain, on the March 1935 reconnaissance flight with Bob Randall, when the twenty-four-year-old Brad had shot his first pictures of Lucania. "Randall was so far from home," Brad related now, "that he said, 'I'm lost. Where the hell are we?' I said, 'You just fly the plane, I'll tell you where we are.'"

Suddenly, ahead of us and slightly to the left, we saw Lucania. I recognized it like an old friend of a mountain, though until now I had known it only through Brad's photographs. We came to the junction of the Walsh and Logan Glaciers. As Kelly flew up the Walsh, we crossed the border into Canada. Had Brad and Bob hiked out to McCarthy, the thirty miles between this junction and their base camp would have been the only terra incognita on their escape route. And now, as I gazed down, it was clear that those thirty miles would have been a piece of cake, a stroll on a broad glacier uncomplicated by icefalls or serious crevasse fields.

We were a good 3,000 feet above the glacier, gaining height so that we could pop over the Steele-Lucania ridge and push on to the east. Off my window, the gargantuan south face of Lucania slowly unveiled itself, in the late morning sun almost too bright to look at. We came to a corner where the Walsh bent toward the north. "Where was your base camp, Brad?" I asked.

He leaned across the pilot and counted with his right index finger: "One, two, three ribs—just off the third rib." I spotted the rocky spurs pitching off the south face, but we were too high to make out any details near the foot of the third one. On the way back, we would fly low to check out the terrain more carefully. Now, just off the wing lay the headwall Brad and Bob had fought so hard to carry their loads up. In the fresh snow, I saw small slide runnels everywhere on that slope. It was obvious why the two men had worried about getting avalanched there.

Kelly circled within the basin to gain altitude. "We got fourteen-six here," said the pilot, glancing at the altimeter.

"We ought to get over that pass easily," said Brad. "It's about fourteen."

Kelly preferred a little insurance. We circled up to 15,500 feet, near the limit for a Cessna 185. I felt light-headed in the thin air. "I've never had it over sixteen," Kelly admitted. "But it's got a brand new engine in it."

"Good!" exclaimed Barbara, clutching her down jacket.

In a sudden swoop, we crossed the Steele-Lucania pass. I stared down at the featureless snow, where sixty-four years before, Brad and Bob had pitched their tent triumphantly at Shangri-La. "We had a hell of a good camp here," Brad told Kelly. "No cracks anywhere." Within minutes, we were descending the far side of Steele, with the northeast ridge on our left. It looked alarmingly steep and sharp. Brad gazed down at the Wolf Creek Glacier (now officially named the Steele Glacier). "Boy, that would be good walking down there," he said.

A flight such as the one we were taking, I knew, ran the risk of trivializing the experience it was designed to appreciate. Here we were, after all, floating in comfort inside a heated cabin across terrain that Brad and Bob had had to fight for, foot by foot and day by day. Yet so far, the flight had only deepened my respect for their journey. In particular, the sheer hugeness of Lucania came home to me: only McKinley, among the mountains I had climbed, was in the same league.

We followed the glacier down, until it bent slightly toward the right. "There's Peter Rabbit corner!" Brad cried, pointing at a grassy bench on the right bank. He told the pilot the story of finding Walter Wood's cache, ruined by bears except for the single small jar of Peter Rabbit peanut butter. Kelly shook his head. "You can throttle back here and save gas," Brad advised. "Just glide down to the Donjek."

We had enough fuel for about a four-hour flight. The Donjek would make a safe turnaround point. We would not be able to fly the last thirty miles to Burwash Landing, but after all, Brad and Bob had ridden horses on that last, uneventful leg.

We lost altitude as the valley gentled. The perfect day was holding. I realized that since we had turned up the Walsh Glacier, I had been in the grips of a strange mood, a mixture of elation and agitation. During the previous months, I had so relived Brad and Bob's 1937 adventure that it was almost as if now I were retracing an old voyage of my own. And at the moment, with sparkling streams pouring off the green hillsides in full summer, I wanted to be down there, hiking toward my future.

"There's the Donjek!" Brad exclaimed. Slowly we approached it, until you could count the silver braids in the current.

"Donjek's a pretty big river," mused Kelly, who had seldom flown so far east of his backyard.

"It's a son of a bitch," said Brad.

We turned south to fly upstream, heading for the snout of the Donjek Glacier, where Brad and Bob had passed the most miserable and anxious night of their lives.

Brad saw it before I did. "The glacier's surging!" he cried. I stared out my window. The Donjek Glacier, pouring out of the foothills to the west, sprawled into the river from an oblique angle. But where, in 1937, the main current of the river had torn viciously through a canyon carved between rock cliffs on the east and the glacial snout on the west, we saw that now the glacier lay completely athwart the river. The main current of the river, pouring from its true source in the Kluane Glacier fifteen miles farther south, had carved a tunnel beneath the snout of the Donjek. "Yes," said Brad, who knew his geology, "that glacier's advancing to beat the band."

All glaciers flow downhill at a rate of inches or feet per year. But in a still little-understood phenomenon, glaciers may unaccountably surge, galloping forward by hundreds of yards per year for a brief span of time. Though glaciers everywhere in the Yukon and Alaska have for the most part retreated steadily during the last century, as melting outstrips their downhill flow, sometime within the past sixty-four years the Donjek had surged, so that its terminus now completely crossed the river.

"We could have just walked over on the ice!" Brad groaned. Barbara patted him on the shoulder.

It was time to turn around. As we headed back toward Mount Steele, I reflected that any lingering doubts I had had about Brad and Bob's crucial rationalization, that to head east toward Kluane Lake was the best way to go to get out of the Saint Elias Range, had vanished. There was absolutely no chance that the hundred-mile hike west to McCarthy would have proved tougher than Brad and Bob's eventual 156-mile flight to Burwash. I would guess, to the contrary, that a trek down the Walsh, Logan, and Chitina Glaciers and then down the Chitina valley would have been three or four times safer and easier than what Brad and Bob ended up performing. But in that case, of course, they would have had to leave the first ascent of Lucania to someone else.

We crossed back over the Steele-Lucania Ridge. Kelly circled over the Walsh Glacier to lose altitude. It had been Brad's hope (and mine) that we might catch a glimpse of the base camp cache the men had abandoned on June 26, 1937. No other climbers had ever reported its discovery, but even by 2001, very few men or women had penetrated to the upper basin of the Walsh. As Kelly now said, "The truth of it is, there aren't a heck of a lot of people that have ever looked around up here."

Indeed, I felt stunned by the emptiness of the wilderness we had flown over during the last two and a half hours. At that moment, on Denali's West Buttress, probably two or three hundred climbers were scattered up and down the route, their tents and gear caches littering the slopes. The weather was so good that maybe a dozen or two were at that very instant hugging each other and snapping pictures on the summit. But I was quite sure that in the 120-mile swath of Saint

Elias Range we had surveyed, not a single human being was presently abroad. The Lucania region seemed as unexplored as it had been in 1937.

Only two hundred feet above the glacier, Kelly straightened out and took the line Brad indicated. Brad peered out the right front window, I out the left rear. Kelly slowed the Cessna to about a hundred miles an hour. A skin of snow still coated the glacier, but we saw meltwater pools and rivulets.

There was no question of landing: Kelly had no planes on skis in midsummer, and he was not authorized to make glacier landings in Canada. With our eyes, we scoured the landscape whizzing by beneath us, but we saw nothing but snow and a long ribbon of morainal gravel on the dirty ice. Brad turned to me and said, "You know what we should do? Come back here with a helicopter, land, and just walk down that moraine." I had no doubt that, had Kelly been able to land, Brad would have hopped out the door and headed off unroped down-glacier to look for his lost cache.

Less than half a mile in a direct line below the site of that long-ago camp, the glacier slumped into a chaotic jumble of crevasses and toppled séracs. It seemed to me that here was the likely answer: with the flow of the decades, all Bob and Brad's precious gear had most likely been dumped into this frozen maelstrom, where it now lay entombed in ice. I didn't have the heart to say as much to Brad.

We rose again and headed for McCarthy. No one said anything for ten or fifteen minutes. I felt a bittersweet longing come over my spirits.

I had expected that the flight would stir in Brad a kindred pang. Late in life, an old story has it, the British writer

Jonathan Swift was asked for the umpteenth time whether he had indeed penned the anonymously published *A Tale of a Tub,* a work so brilliantly heretical it might well have landed its author in prison. For the umpteenth time, Swift denied the attribution. But then he turned and muttered to himself, in a barely audible voice, "Ah, what a genius I had in me then!"

Surely our flight over Lucania had awakened in Brad some nostalgic sorrow, some fresh cognizance of the glory of youth slipping away irretrievably into the past. But if Brad had such feelings in his breast, he kept them to himself.

We flew past the snout of a nameless glacier joining the Logan from the south side. Brad pointed: "Each one of those lobes there marks a different glacial surge." As the plane sped on, he stared back, caught up in his geology. "Isn't that interesting?" he said. His breath whistled softly in the headphone. "I'll be darned."

A C K N O W L E D G M E N T S

THIS book, of course, would not exist without Bob Bates and Brad Washburn. My longtime admiration for the feat they pulled off in the Yukon Territory in 1937 was deepened, during the last two years, by my gratitude for their willingness to reminisce at length in front of my tape recorder, as well as to allow a person who had not even been born when they attacked Mount Lucania to tell in print what was after all a very personal story. Brad, in particular, saw more than a decade ago that Lucania deserved a book, and was kind enough to think that I might be the person who should write it.

By sharing their husbands' adventures decade after decade, and by resolutely backing them through the most unlikely and perilous of projects, Gail Bates and Barbara Washburn have each helped construct that rarest of modern edifices, a happy marriage. Bob and Brad have often, in slide shows and lectures as well as in print, expressed their own gratitude to and appreciation of Gail and Barbara. May I here add my own, for both women encouraged me from start to finish.

When I was in my early twenties, setting out to be a mountaineer myself, Bob and Brad gave me all the support and advice I could have hoped for. As such, the two men were part of a sizable cadre of members of the Harvard Mountaineering Club, dating back to its founding in 1924, who served as role models and mentors to my generation in the early 1960s. To them, and to the cronies with whom I set off on my own expeditions to Alaska and the Yukon, I owe some of the best friendships and unquestionably the greatest adventures of my life.

Jon Krakauer and Sharon Roberts read my book in manuscript and gave me many valuable tips. Kelly and Natalie Bay, of Wrangell Mountain Air, did some slick flying to allow Brad, Barbara, and me to retrace by airplane the route of the 1937 escape from Lucania on the finest day of the summer of 2001. The Bays are classic Alaskan bush pilots in the tradition of which Bob Reeve was one of the pioneers; he would have been proud of them.

To my agent, Stuart Krichevsky, I owe not only the professional acumen that allowed my book to become a reality, but an abiding interest in the story that transcended our mere business relationship. The same holds true for Shana Cohen, Stuart's associate, who untangled many a logistical snag while always expressing her enthusiasm for the Lucania saga. Stuart and Shana even served as my part-time research assistants, hunting down such arcana as the ur-texts of *Tillie the Toiler*.

At Simon & Schuster, Johanna Li once more, in her apparently effortless way, kept track of all the loose ends that every book seems to come booby-trapped with. If there is a better associate editor than Johanna in American publishing, I'd be surprised. I have lost track of the numbers of colleagues who, as we faced some apparently unprecedented dilemma in writing, research, or permissions, said to me over the phone, "I'll call Johanna—she'll know how to straighten this out."

Finally, on this, my sixth book for Simon & Schuster, Bob Bender has once more proved the ideal custodian of my prose. It is a rare occasion when one's editor becomes a true friend, and rarer still when the most discerning critical judgment on the editor's part coexists with that friendship. Bob, after all, would not be doing his job if he did not save me from the flights of rhetorical excess and trudges of expository plod that every writer lapses into now and then. All I can hope is that, no matter for how many years I continue to scribble away, I never have another editor than Bob Bender.

I N D E X